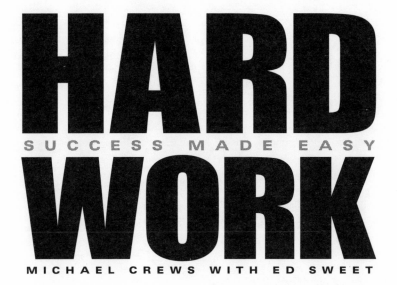

HARD

SUCCESS MADE EASY

WORK

MICHAEL CREWS WITH ED SWEET

HENRY COOPER
BUSINESS BOOKS

Phoenix

Henry Cooper Business Books are published by Henry Cooper Press,
P.O. Box 97126, Phoenix, AZ 85060-7126

Visit our Web site at **henrycooperpress.com.**

Books are available in quantity for educational, promotional, or premium use.
For information on discounts and terms, call **888-861-2600** or write to
sales@henrycooperpress.com.

Michael Crews is available for motivational speaking engagements.
To make arrangements, please write to **michaelc@michaelcrews.com**
or call **760-749-1919.**

Publisher's Cataloging-in-Publication
(Provided by Quality Books, Inc.)
    Crews, Michael.
    Hard work : success made easy / Michael Crews with Ed
Sweet. -- 1st ed.
    p. cm.
    Includes index.
    LCCN 2003112996
    ISBN 0-9743304-0-X

    1. Success in business. 2. Crews, Michael.
I. Sweet, Ed. II. Title.
    HF5386.C895 2004   650.1
                        QBI03-200766

Printed in the United States of America

First Printing: April 2004

10 9 8 7 6 5 4 3 2 1

Book design by Michele DeFilippo/1106 Design
Jacket by Campbell Fisher Design
Cover photo by Garrett Delph/Garrett Photography

As I note in these pages,
hard work is made out of love.
This book is the fruit of both.
Many people have influenced this work,
but none more so than my wife Kelly.

Her willingness to read and re-read
every draft, her insightful suggestions,
and her ability to bring out the best in me
have made this book possible.

Kelly, I thank you for fulfilling my life
and unselfishly supporting my dreams.

*This book is dedicated
to the people who fill my life
with joy and purpose:*

My beautiful wife, Kelly

*My incredible children,
Ashley, Tyler, Justin, Sky, and Jet*

My loving parents, Ken and Erlene

*And all my hardworking co-workers
and wonderful customers—
past, present, and future*

Contents

Foreword

The first thing I remember about Michael Crews is something that happened during a high school football game. I think it was the first time we ever played together as Orange Glen Patriots. Besides being a wide receiver, and a pretty good one at that, Michael played center whenever we had to punt the ball. I was the kicker, and I was getting ready to punt. Michael snapped the ball at me, and up it went, way over my head toward the end zone. I had to hustle like crazy to grab the ball!

Despite such inauspicious beginnings, Michael and I became good friends. We both loved athletics, and we also had another thing in common—neither of us would ever be accused of being the smartest guy in school. Michael was a year older than me, and after he graduated we still saw each other now and then. In fact, at one point Michael worked for my dad, who built houses for a living.

By the time I graduated from high school in 1975, I was working for my dad and Michael was a real estate agent, selling houses. He worked hard at it, and I remember seeing his name on quite a few of the Forest E. Olson signs in front of houses in Escondido, California, our home town.

Several years later, I got a call from Michael, kind of out of the blue. He told me that he had just bought a house, and that he needed to have it moved to another piece of property. I swear I thought he was pulling my leg, but he was persistent. Finally, I agreed to take a look. He took me over to the house and it seemed okay, but I still thought he was nuts to have purchased a house that had to be moved.

Somehow, he convinced me to help him figure out how to move this house. Like it was yesterday, I can still remember being on the road, drinking a Dr. Pepper, driving behind the truck that carried this house to its new location. Neither of us could really believe it was happening. But then again, we were 24 years old and couldn't believe that it wouldn't all work out, either.

We moved the house, fixed it up, sold it within 45 days, and split the profits. I think we each made about $20,000. We had a good time, we made some money, and, since neither of us really had anything else to do, we decided to do it again. And again. And again.

We liked working together and soon we were building houses from scratch. I managed the design and construction, and Michael found the land, ran around with the city, and did the selling. To his credit, he helped out with a lot of the building, too. I remember many days when we were both high up on sticks, hammering nails in the Southern California sun. We did as much as we could by ourselves, and my dad helped us out by talking to his bankers on our behalf.

We did whatever it took to make it, and we stayed focused on our goals. We didn't spend our money on vacations or other frivolous things. We were working so hard, we didn't have the time!

From the beginning, we decided to put out a product that was good. We saw a need for quality houses that our friends could afford, and our mission in those early days was to build the best house that $80,000 could buy. Our friends and other young people appreciated this, and our business did pretty well. As we grew, so did our projects, and we ended up selling a lot of bigger houses to the same people we had previously sold small houses to.

It was fun and exciting, and Michael and I worked together for 12 years before I decided that it was time for me to do something different. Frankly, I was getting a little burnt out from all the rules and regulations being placed on home builders by city officials and environmentalists. But Michael's such a positive, upbeat guy that nothing brings him down. He stayed on and continues to run an incredibly successful development business on his own.

We still work together, too, just in different ways. Our friendship is one of those rare gifts that only come around once in a lifetime, if you're lucky. If I could trust anyone with anything, it would be Michael Crews. He's a hardworking person with a vision and drive to be the best that most people just don't have.

Michael has a million great qualities, but the thing that really comes to mind when I think about why he's gotten so far in so short a time is his ability to make quick decisions. He doesn't hesitate or wait. He's confident enough in himself and in the way the world works to jump on opportunities before they get away.

That's not to say that things have always worked out for Michael Crews. I remember really busting our butts for six months on two or three little houses when we were just getting started as business owners, and barely breaking even on them because the economy was bad. But setbacks like that never seemed to dampen Michael's spirits. He knew that he couldn't win 100% of the time, but he also knew that hard work brings success in the long run.

His formula for success has always been a simple, yet effective one—find a good deal, use your brain, work hard, learn from your mistakes, and slowly take on larger and larger projects. This formula served Michael and me well in the world of work, but it also did something that we didn't even realize was happening.

Michael and I grew financially, which is what we initially wanted, but we also grew personally and spiritually. As we worked harder and achieved more, we became better people, and as our own lives were enriched, we found pleasure in enriching the lives of others. It started out with our employees and our customers, who we needed to help us build our business. And it extended out to our families, friends, and even to the larger community. Michael Crews calls this continuous process of growth and improvement "upbuilding," and I can vouch for its power to make a positive impact on many, many lives.

I've seen Michael Crews grow from an ordinary kid who wanted to make something of himself into a man who makes something of everyone around him.

Michael started out by moving a house, and now he moves mountains.

Art Duncan
Austin, Texas
2003

What Is Hard Work?

"MICHAEL CREWS!"

I recently ran into someone I haven't seen in a long time, and got a surprisingly enthusiastic reaction.

"You're really, really rich!" the man continued, without even giving me a chance to say hello.

I was taken aback by his abrupt comment, but I thought about it for a second, and realized he was right.

"I *am* really, really rich," I said. "But only because so many people love me!"

H ard work isn't what you think it is. It's more about love than it is about money and material possessions.

Hard work is about loving yourself enough to be the best you can be. It's about loving the people you work with enough to be an effective team player who performs well so that everyone else can succeed, too. It's about loving your customers enough to do the best job you possibly can for their satisfaction. It's about loving your family enough to provide them with the best of what life has to offer. And it's about loving humanity enough to make a difference for people in need.

Hard work is about using your abilities for purposes greater than yourself. You may get rich in the process, and, if you're a real hard worker, you'll use much of the wealth you generate to help others.

Hard work is a precious gift. If you're able to work hard, generate income for yourself, and enrich the lives of your co-workers, customers, and community, then success will surely be yours.

It was a bold decision to call this book *Hard Work*, because the term has such negative connotations. Many people equate hard work with being taken advantage of. Many people believe the misconception that the only people who work hard are poor, exploited workers who break their backs making other people, who don't work hard, rich.

Well, I'm on a mission to change how people feel about hard work. I'm on a mission to show people how positive hard work can be, and how it can create a future of incredible ease and enjoyment. I'm out to change people's minds about hard work so that more people can benefit from all the riches and rewards it has to offer.

Since I started writing this book, I hear more and more people talking about the value of hard work, and that makes me very happy. I think that hard work is making a comeback in the U.S., and I think that the timing for this book is right on target.

Look around you and really observe the most successful people you can find. Nearly all of them talk about hard work if you listen closely. I'm not a big talk radio fan—I don't have time to listen!—but people tell me that successful personalities like Sean Hannity are always singing the praises of hard work to millions of listeners on a daily basis. There was a time when the popular singer James Brown made his reputation as "the hardest-working man in show business."

Hard work is part of our American mythology. Corporate America is filled with stories of CEOs who worked their way up from the mail room, tireless inventors who overcame incredible obstacles to realize their visions, immigrants who came to this country with nothing and built great fortunes, and maverick entrepreneurs who continually change the face of business. I've started reading a lot of motivational business books and biographies lately, and the hard-work theme comes up again and again—even if the authors are afraid to broadcast that message on their covers.

Well, I'm not afraid. I'm not afraid to tell people how valuable and rewarding hard work can be. I'm not afraid to tell my story, which is just one of many in this country that proves that hard work can make anyone a success.

If you follow the system of hard work that I explain in this book, I can practically guarantee that you'll have a rich and rewarding career. If you apply the same lessons I've learned about work to your own situation, then you too can find joy through a productive contribution to society and keep rising to greater levels of achievement and success.

When I was starting out, all I wanted was to make a lot of money. I wanted to be better than everyone else, and I wanted the income to prove it. I still enjoy winning and making money, but money for its own sake is no longer my top priority. Today, my top priority is using the money I earn to make my businesses the best places to work, make the world a better place to live, and turn as many people as I can into successful hard workers.

I'm not going to lie to you. Hard work is hard work. But after awhile, it becomes effortless. Hard work lifts you up instead of wearing you down. And after all is said and done, it truly is the easy way to achieve the success you desire.

My goal in writing *Hard Work* is to inspire you to go for your dreams and to give you a step-by-step method of working hard that you can use to easily achieve success. You've got nothing to lose and everything to gain by following this program. To be honest with you, if I had known how great the rewards of working hard were going to be when I was first starting out, I would have worked a thousand times harder than I did.

I want you to take the time you're allotted on this planet and really make something of your life. You're here anyway, so why not work hard and do something great?

This book is intended for anyone who wants to find joy, purpose, and success in his or her work and career. It's just as relevant for entry-level employees and recent high school and college graduates as it is for seasoned senior managers and pioneering entrepreneurs. *Hard Work* is for everyone who works for a living.

Plus, as an extra bonus, when you start following the suggestions I'm going to give you for working hard in the business world, you'll also find that the principles apply just as well to your personal relationships.

Hard Work is part memoir and part do-it-yourself guide to success. Every chapter begins with a different story from my life. Some of the stories are from my childhood, some are from my career, and some are about my family and friends. All of the stories throughout the book are about people and events that have shaped my work ethic. Living through these experiences has helped me develop a philosophy of success that finds great pleasure in working hard, and I hope that sharing them with you will help you find joy and success in your own career.

Hard Work is populated with some pretty amazing people. You'll meet Luis Feria, who I literally found underneath an orange tree and who is now an integral part of my team of trusted managers. You'll meet my son, Justin, who decided to follow his dad's approach to business and at 19 is already profiting from his hard work. You'll meet Norma Eckblad, an inspiring woman who refused to let cancer ruin the business she built with her husband. And you'll meet my wife, my parents, and some of the many teachers, coaches, bosses, co-workers, and customers who've had a profound impact on my success.

Hard Work is divided into three parts, all of which I hope will give you valuable insights you can use immediately at your current job, and then throughout your career as you advance toward bigger goals and dreams.

In Part I, you'll learn an awful lot about Michael Crews. I'll tell you how I overcame my weaknesses and learned to play to my strengths. It's an honest and straightforward account of my personal history, from my early days growing up in rural California to when I started getting my career in full gear. You'll read about my struggle with school and how I rose above my academic shortcomings. You'll learn how my experiences playing team sports gave me the spirit to compete in business and be the best "coach" I can possibly be to my co-workers. You'll see how my parents taught me the value of hard work, integrity, love, and respect. And you'll discover how I built my career from making $2.80 an hour to generating more than $100 million a year.

You'll learn how good values helped a kid who didn't get very good grades, and who, in the opinion of many so-called authority figures, didn't have much of a chance in life. Because I had a solid foundation, I was able to make choices that allowed me to succeed when it would have been incredibly easy for me to fail.

In Part II, I discuss why I think hard work is so important if you want to be a success in business and in life. You'll see how hard work can not only bring you incredible financial gain, but also how it can bring purpose, joy, and good times to your life, how it can enrich the lives of your co-workers and the customers of your business, and how it can bring unexpected benefits to the larger community.

In Part III, you'll read about specific hard-work actions you can start taking immediately to help you get ahead. These are the actions to which I credit my success, and I believe they can help you achieve remarkable things if you apply them faithfully and consistently at your place of business.

Although I believe deeply that the cornerstone of success is hard work, I also know that I've been very lucky in life. I've been blessed with wonderful parents who nurtured me and taught me the importance of good character. I've been blessed with wonderful coaches who inspired me to give 150% because winning as a team felt so good. I've been blessed with wonderful friends like Art Duncan, who wrote the foreword to this book and who was willing to take a chance with me when we were both starting out. And I've been blessed with wonderful co-workers and customers who continue to build me up more than they'll ever realize, and who constantly inspire me to work harder and harder.

I hope this book contains everything you need to succeed. I hope it gives you all kinds of ideas on how to improve your position in the business world, whether you're just starting out or whether you're a work-force veteran.

I'll be honest with you. This isn't one of those get-rich-quick or work-less-earn-more types of books. It won't give you unrealistic expectations that ultimately make you feel like a failure when you don't make your first million dollars overnight. And it's not a book about making money in real estate, although, as a real estate developer, I can't help but include a few tips about buying and selling houses in the story of my life, now can I?

Hard Work is a book that celebrates the fundamental truth about business that it takes effort to achieve goals. In celebrating this truth, the book reveals that the effort you expend can actually make life easier and more effortless than you ever thought possible—not only for yourself, but also for your family, your friends, your co-workers, your customers, and countless others in the larger community.

You'll learn that working hard is, in the long run, a lot easier than complaining about work, getting mad at people or problems, and otherwise wasting time that could be spent reaching your goals and dreams and actually achieving the success you desire. Hard work doesn't have to be difficult. Hard work can be the easy way to achieve success.

These ideas aren't new—America is great because it gives all of us the freedom to be hard workers. We all know that hard work works.

But somewhere along the line, many Americans have become less willing to work hard. Many people buy into the idea that hard work is for suckers and that there are faster, easier ways to success. Multi-million-dollar lottery jackpots, the dot-com phenomenon, popular infomercials, and million-dollar game shows and reality shows tell us that instant gratification and wealth through non-work is possible. While this may be true, it's dangerous to believe that this is a better way to get ahead. Frankly, it scares me to see this belief taking over the minds of kids today, who seem to have very little drive—and no idea how—to really do something satisfying and meaningful with their lives.

And yet, I truly believe that Americans are ready to get back to basics when it comes to business success. I think people are getting tired of being told that they can be a one-minute manager, make a fast buck, or that they should step all over people in a race to the top of the corporate ladder. I believe that people are ready to do a little hard work.

I offer my story as proof that you can do things that, deep down, you know you're capable of. You can run a successful business. You can be a manager who gets incredible results from a team of people who respect your leadership and love to come to work in the morning. Or you can be one of those wonderful employees who relish their work and see each day as a new opportunity to do something great. No matter where you are or what you want out of your career, you can lead yourself and others to greatness through a set of very simple and doable actions that revolve around one central theme—hard work.

PART I

How I Became A Hard Worker

MY DAD AND I WERE OUTSIDE in the garden. He was thinning out a flowerbed.

I was walking around, giggling, enjoying life–all the usual things that 18-month-olds do when they're outside on a beautiful sunny morning with their dads.

My dad kept a watchful eye out for me, but he was also pretty focused on what he was doing. I watched him intently as he pulled out weeds, leaves, and some of the unhealthy flowers so the healthy ones would have a better chance to grow.

I continued to take it all in as my dad collected all the things he pulled out of the flowerbed and put them into a garbage can.

My dad had to run into the house for a minute, and he left me in charge of the garden. I decided to finish the job he started, and proceeded to pull out the rest of the flowers.

I was just about to throw them in the vague direction of the garbage can by the time my dad came back outside.

"Michael, what have you done!" he exclaimed.

My dad was frustrated that I ruined his flowerbed, but his initial reaction soon gave way to a certain pride in his son's achievement. A hardworking man himself, I think my dad was impressed by my initiative—as misguided as it was.

A smile soon crossed my dad's face after I looked up at him, wondering what I could possibly have done wrong.

He picked me up and held me high up in the sky, and I smiled back at him—happy to have helped him out.

The little episode in the flowerbed told my dad that he had a son who was observant, focused, and willing to work at getting the job done. From that day on, both of my parents knew that I'd be able to find my way in the world.

Today, I work hard at building houses. I've probably built more than 2,500 houses in North San Diego County, California, the place where I grew up.

But then again, I knew that I was going to be pretty good at it when I got started. Not because of arrogance, but because of commitment. All I had when I was growing up was a desire to make something of myself. Success was what I wanted more than anything else in the world. My desire to succeed in life was so deep that I was willing to do whatever it took to achieve my goals. I've worked as hard or harder than anyone I know.

The longer I continued working hard, the easier it was for me to achieve greater successes. Hard work has never been drudgery for me, because I always knew that it was the one thing I could do to make money, get recognition and praise, fulfill a purpose for my life, and help other people at the same time.

As hard as I worked, however, I was careful never to bite off more than I could chew. I always started with small projects, so I could learn from my mistakes and not put too much at risk at any one time. Then, as I got more skilled and confident, I could apply the things I learned to bigger projects over time.

Looking back on my early days, that's kind of how I built my whole career, even before I started building houses. I'd work hard and do the best I could at whatever I was doing, and keep looking for ways to make small improvements that would lead to greater achievements.

Being patient and methodical wasn't always what I wanted to be doing, but I'm convinced that I would never have become so successful if I had followed a different strategy. I consider myself fortunate that the foundation for this type of behavior was solidly laid down in my childhood and was continually reinforced by my parents and coaches in school.

Today, I'm the one setting the example, primarily in my role as the leader of a company called Michael Crews Development. I'm the one helping people develop the kind of work habits that allow them to succeed in their jobs, have fun doing what they're doing, and take pride in even the smallest tasks. I always try to give the people I work with whatever they need to do their jobs as best as they can. I expect them to work hard, and I reward them for their efforts. And I always try to help them reach their full potential by trusting in their abilities and giving them more responsibility.

So while I work hard at building houses for a living, it's really just the context through which I perform a much more important activity—building people, myself included. It's a pretty simple formula for success, but it really works. When you're willing to work hard consistently over time and always look for new, yet manageable, challenges, you can achieve more in your life and help more people than you ever thought possible.

I always had a great personal drive to succeed in life, but after I graduated from high school I wasn't sure how I was going to make it happen. I tried going to college, but after just four days I realized that it wasn't the right environment for me. In my mind, college was a waste of four years that I could spend working and making money.

My ambition motivated me to work hard and to continually challenge myself to do better and better as an employee, as a manager, and as a business leader. I started out making $2.80 an hour hauling water tanks, and today I'm involved in a dozen or so businesses that generate more than $100 million in sales each year.

As I reached each goal that I set for myself and as my businesses grew, I realized that while working hard and upbuilding myself was a profitable personal technique, upbuilding others was an even more profitable management technique. As I helped the people who worked for me become more confident, skilled, wealthy, happy, and productive, my personal career success grew even more and my goals got bigger and bigger.

I'm not a celebrity or a famous person. I don't run a *Fortune* 500 company. And unless you live in Escondido or Valley Center, California, you've probably never heard of me, or my businesses.

I didn't inherit any money. I didn't win the lottery. I'm definitely not a genius, I'm not particularly photogenic, and although sports got me through high school, I wasn't destined for the pros.

While it would have been easy for me to settle for a mediocre existence, deep down I knew that I could rise above my perceived shortcomings. What many people didn't know about me was that I had a secret weapon.

I was willing to work hard with vision and focus. And as far as I'm concerned, that's pretty big. I had a deep conviction that I could take charge of my own destiny, find a way to make a lot of money, and be productive and successful.

Even when I was making $2.80 an hour delivering water tanks, I always made the best of wherever I was in my career and, at the same time, kept looking for new opportunities and ways to improve my situation.

All of my success has been achieved through good old-fashioned hard work and a firm belief that I could succeed even when other people thought I would fail. When I started managing people, I extended that same positive belief to the people working for me, and that simple technique helped me create exciting, energetic work environments where manager and "managees" were all able to thrive.

These attributes—a strong work ethic and a belief in people's abilities—are available to anybody who can see their value and decide to apply them to their careers. I don't have more hours in the day than anyone else, but by working harder I'm able to get a lot more done each day. By working hard, I don't have time to complain about my job. And by having faith in the other members of my team, I'm a lot less likely to let anger, frustration, or jealousy interfere with getting the job done and more likely to look for opportunities to help myself and all the people I work with succeed.

I don't care where you are in your career. If you commit to working hard you'll make dramatic advances. If you think this isn't true, I'm living proof that it is.

Michael Crews wasn't supposed to succeed. Michael Crews was supposed to remain a laborer working for minimum wage. Michael Crews was supposed to fade away into obscurity, leaving real success to college graduates, the Beautiful People, and kids from the right families.

Now, don't get me wrong. I don't begrudge anybody's success in life, and I want everybody—including college graduates—to work hard, build themselves up, and help others succeed. This type of activity makes the world a better place.

I just don't think that *anybody* should be ruled out when it comes to being successful. To really make it in the world, I believe that the only things you need are a burning desire to get ahead and a willingness to work hard.

I Wasn't Stupid, But School Just Wasn't My Thing

I STOOD IN FRONT OF 30 other third graders and a teacher with a skeptical look on her face.

"One times one is one," I began.

For the last few weeks, we had been learning our multiplication tables. Part of the requirement for passing the lesson was to stand in front of the class and recite all the tables from 1 through 10.

"Two times four is eight," I continued.

Every day, kids would get up in front of the class and recite one or two of the tables as we learned them. We were free to do this whenever we wanted, and the teacher would check off the tables we completed successfully on a big chart hanging in the room for all to see.

"Three times seven is twenty-one."

Getting up in front of my classmates was the last thing I wanted to do, so I kept putting it off. I didn't know the multiplication tables, and

I didn't want to learn them. Whenever the teacher asked who wanted to get up and recite, I slunk down in my chair. As the days progressed, the empty row next to my name on the big chart was becoming more and more conspicuous.

"Six times three is eighteen."

It was the next-to-last day of multiplication when my teacher, Mrs. Penny, called my dad and explained to him that I hadn't gotten up in front of the class yet.

"Eight times five is forty."

My father told Mrs. Penny that I'd recite all ten of the multiplication tables for her the next day. He sat me down after school, made me focus, and made me memorize everything I needed to know. Never before or since that time did my dad come down on me so hard about school.

"Ten times ten is one hundred," I finished.

The students cheered and applauded, and Mrs. Penny was stunned.

"Now that's what you can do when you put your mind to it, Michael," she said with a smile, as she put the final check mark next to my name on the wall chart.

▬▬▬▬▬▬

Reciting those multiplication tables one after another as a nine-year-old wasn't easy, but I did it. And I survived. My dad made me do the work I needed to do, and that helped me overcome my fear of looking foolish in public. I learned that if I worked hard enough, I could achieve things that seemed impossible. I felt good about myself.

Despite this little victory, however, I never really got interested in the things that textbooks had to offer. I had difficulty reading, and I had an incredibly short attention span. I would've been a big-time candidate for Ritalin if they knew about ADD when I was a kid.

But somehow I managed to get through each year and pass each grade. I think part of the reason was that in many ways, even though I never exactly kept up with all my class work, I was a model student. I was always polite and well behaved, I always helped out in the classroom, and I always showed respect to my teachers.

There were also a few school assignments that I was genuinely interested in. On the rare occasions when we got to build things and learn how things worked, I got really excited and engaged—and when I get involved in something, there's no stopping me!

I remember a seventh grade science fair project I worked on that involved hatching chickens from eggs. The result was two pet chickens, first place in the science fair, and the opportunity to build my first house. I learned all about incubation and what type of environment was necessary to get chicken eggs to hatch. I went to 7-Eleven and bought a big Styrofoam cooler, put in a light bulb for heat and a dish of water to create humidity, and even made a window using a picture frame. I kept the "house" in my science teacher's classroom, and every day in science class I'd check on the eggs and rotate them so the heat from the light bulb was evenly distributed.

When the chicks started hatching I was in another part of the school, but I remember five kids running to tell me that I'd better get to the science classroom quick. We all ran back as fast as we could, and I watched as two little chicks introduced themselves to the world. They bonded with me right away, and for years they'd run to me like I was their mother.

Projects that involved making things showed my teachers that I had definite abilities, but when it came to learning from books I felt like I was from a different planet. My reading disability made studying textbooks uncomfortable for me, so I avoided it as much as possible.

My parents wanted me to get good grades and were always helping me with my homework, but they never showed too much concern when my performance was less than spectacular. They knew that I had the strength of character to succeed, which to them was more important than book smarts. They never worried about me when it came to school (at least they never showed it) and I never felt any pressure to do better, except when my dad made me learn all the multiplication tables in one night.

My struggle with academics was more of an issue in high school. I was heavily involved in athletics and played three different marquee sports—baseball, football, and basketball. I loved team sports more than anything, and I honestly thought I was going to become a professional athlete. Who needed algebra, chemistry, or English literature?

Unfortunately, I did. If I wanted to play sports at Orange Glen High School, I had to pass all my classes. So I just did what I had to do in school to play sports. I got mostly Cs and a couple of Ds, but it was good enough for me to stay on my teams and keep playing the sports I loved so much.

I got through my freshman and sophomore years without a problem, but an interesting thing happened when I was a junior. I was failing geometry. If I got an F in geometry I couldn't play sports, and let me tell you, there was no way around the fact that I was getting an F in geometry.

Somebody must have been looking out for me, however, because it turned out that the geometry teacher was also the boy's track coach at Orange Glen High School. He made me a proposition. He told me that if I'd run track instead of play baseball that year, he'd give me a C in geometry.

I ran track that year and I even did pretty well. I competed in all the sprinting events—the 100-yard dash, the 220, and the 440 relay. I had never really run competitively before, but I was the second fastest guy on the team. I still have it out for Bob Peavey, the one guy in the entire school who was faster than I was.

Looking back on the whole experience, I admit that I didn't make the most ethical decision I could have made. But I was 16 or 17 years old and pretty pragmatic. When senior year rolled around and I didn't have to worry about grades interfering with my eligibility for sports, I played baseball again and had a great season with my old teammates.

I did, however, have a run-in with a math teacher during my senior year that had a big impact on me. One day, after he handed back one of our tests, he asked me to stay after class.

"What is it, Mr. Sowers?" I asked respectfully, eager to get to baseball practice.

"You know you're failing my class," he said.

I suppose I knew it, but to be honest I wasn't really thinking about it. After all, I was a senior and failing a class wouldn't prevent me from participating in sports anymore, or from graduating. But I was polite. "I know, sir. I'm not very good at math."

"That's the understatement of the year," he said. "Don't you realize that you need mathematics to get through life? Don't you realize that if you don't pass my class, you'll never amount to anything?"

That stung. It hit hard. I couldn't believe he was actually saying these things to me. I couldn't believe that he was condemning me to a future as a good-for-nothing loser, just because I was failing a math class. Maybe he didn't mean it that way, but that's how I took it.

As calmly and as respectfully as I could, I told Mr. Sowers that I wouldn't need the information he was teaching in order to be a success in life.

Two years after I graduated from high school, when I was selling houses for a living, I ran into Mr. Sowers on the street. The first thing he did was apologize to me. He told me that he saw all my real estate signs in the community and imagined that I must have been doing pretty well, despite getting an F in his class. He told me that he was proud of me.

I can't tell you how much that meant to me. I accepted his apology with gratitude, and I asked Mr. Sowers a favor. I asked him not to say anything negative to a kid again. I think he learned the lesson on his own, but I thought it was worth reinforcing—because, as the saying goes, one negative requires at least ten positives just to break even.

I still see Mr. Sowers to this very day and we've become good friends. He's very active in the community and is one of the most generous, giving guys you'd ever want to meet. We often joke about his comment to me about not amounting to anything in life.

I believe that school is great for some people, but it's not the answer for everybody. It certainly wasn't the answer for me. Parents need to realize that it's not the end of the world if their kids don't get all As, as long as they have other qualities and abilities that will serve them well in the future. My parents knew that I was good with my hands. They knew that I was good at sports and loved to play on teams. They knew that I was willing to work hard. My parents were aware of the fact that I was polite, friendly, persuasive, and could carry on a conversation with anyone, and they knew that I was pretty smart when it came to the things I was interested in.

Not all kids are book smart. Some kids are musical. Some kids are artistic. Some kids are athletic. Some kids are funny. Some kids are natural salespeople. Some kids are even too smart for school. Think of Albert Einstein, Thomas Edison, and other great minds who never did well in the classroom. It takes all kinds to make a world, and all kinds can become valuable contributors to society—and successes in their own right.

I believe that parents should worry more about making their kids good people than they do about making them good students. Kids should be appreciated for the things they can do well, not scolded, punished, or labeled as failures for the things they can't do well.

I went to college for four days before I said to myself, "What am I doing here? I don't need this!" The academic system was holding me back, and it wasn't offering me anything that I needed to succeed in life. I wasn't going to be a doctor, or a lawyer, or an accountant, or anything else that required any kind of degree.

While college is necessary for lots of jobs, I don't believe that everybody has to go to college to be successful. Some kids are forced to go, and other kids go because they don't know what else to do. A better strategy, in my opinion, would be for students to work for awhile until they decided what they really wanted to do with their lives. Then, if their chosen path required a college degree, they could pursue it with the same focus and determination as any hard worker. To me, that makes more sense than drifting through college taking classes that may never be of value.

Higher education can be a valuable tool for hard workers, but it's not a requirement for success. School can't teach kids all the skills they might need as they make their way in the world. But school can create a lot of pressure and anxiety for kids who are struggling, and it can also be a place for kids to hide out and waste time when they don't want to face the realities of life.

My love of sports motivated me to stay in school and get my high school diploma, which I believe was a good thing to do. But after my graduation, after I left the halls of academia for good, I was able to really focus on who I was and what I wanted to do with my life. I knew that school just wasn't my thing, and when I was finally done with it, I took off like a shot.

2

My Parents Gave Me
The Tools To Succeed

MY DAD WAS GOING TO FEDMART, and he was taking me with him.

"Mike! You ready yet!?" he hollered.

"Coming dad!" I yelled back.

It was a real treat to go somewhere with my dad, and I was particularly excited that day because I had saved up enough money to get a BB gun. I was 10 years old.

I don't remember what my dad needed at the store, but I do remember him stopping to pick up a couple packets of squash seeds. They were five cents each. He put them in his shirt pocket, and we continued shopping.

I was shooting air BBs all the way back from the store, and I couldn't wait to get home and start using the gun for real. The eight miles from FedMart to our house seemed endless.

When we got home, I was all over my dad to show me how to use my gun and do some shooting with me. My dad worked really hard all week and even on the weekends, so to have him all to myself like this was pretty rare.

My dad felt the seed packets in his pocket. A look of genuine embarrassment and disbelief crossed his face.

"Son, I stole these squash seeds," he said, obviously disappointed with himself. "We've got to go back to the store and pay for them."

All I wanted to do was have my dad show me how to use my BB gun, but I could tell that going back and paying the 10 cents for the squash seeds was a lot more important.

The lesson in honesty and integrity that I learned when my dad went back to pay for 10 cents worth of seeds has stuck with me my entire life, and I apply it to my business every day. As far as I'm concerned, honesty is the best policy in the workplace.

My parents taught me many valuable lessons in character as I was growing up. They're probably the greatest people alive. Okay, so maybe I'm a little biased, but I do credit them with giving me the important tools and values I needed to become a success. Simply put, they raised me right. They taught me all the things that I could never have learned in school.

My mother, Erlene Crews, was the more nurturing of my two parents. She clearly saw the big picture and always had an optimistic attitude, no matter what setbacks, fears, or obstacles she faced. My dad, Ken Crews, was always there for me with the tactical lessons of right and wrong, of what to do and what not to do. I don't know if they planned it that way or if it's just the natural order of things, but they each gave me the best of what they had to offer, and their two parental management styles complemented each other nicely.

Mom always knew that I would do great in life. She recently told me a story about something that happened when I was three years old; an isolated incident that told her I had a pretty good head on my shoulders. My dad had just gotten a job managing duplex apartments, and he moved our whole family into the complex. My mom wanted to put a fence around our yard to keep me from wandering off, so my dad bought a little chain link fence, put it around the yard, and installed a gate. I watched him do his work, and the very next day I got my little hands on a screwdriver and took the gate apart. That told my mom that I was a pretty good problem solver.

My mom went out of her way to make me feel like I was somebody special. She worked hard to provide me with a safe and fulfilling childhood, even though I was able to get out of some of the fences she put up to protect me. She even encouraged my interest in sports, despite the fact that she couldn't stand to watch me play football because she was so nervous about my getting hurt. The fact that she let me play—even though she worried so much and could never bring herself to accompany my dad to my games—really showed me how much she loved me.

My mom had a lot of love to give, and she lavished it on my sister and me. She was the kind of mom everyone dreams of having. In fact, a friend of mine practically lived at our house when we were growing up because my mom was so incredibly nurturing to him.

Neither one of my parents was very strict with me, but that's probably because they instilled good values in me from a very early age. I was a pretty well-behaved kid. My mom showed me that love overcame a lot more difficulties than anger ever did. And my dad taught me rules of behavior that prevented me from testing my mom's philosophy too often!

The lessons my dad taught me served me well in my childhood, and they would also serve me well as I ventured out on my own into the world of business.

One important thing my dad taught me was to show respect for my elders. It started with him and my mom and was extended to my teachers, my coaches, and then to my early employers.

Being courteous and polite was a simple enough thing to do, but it really made me stand out. And although it couldn't make me better at academics, it sure scored some points with many of my teachers.

I brought this lesson with me throughout my career, and I've learned to treat everyone I encounter with respect—not just people who are older than I am. When you're respectful to people and it's sincere, everyone relaxes. Being respectful allows for dialog, minimizes anger and frustration, and fosters trust. Being respectful allows you to cut through a lot of BS and get a lot more work done.

When it came to work, no one worked harder than my dad. Probably the biggest lesson he ever taught me was how to work. I hire kids today and I'm amazed at how many of them just don't know how to work. They often have no concept of what it means to focus on a task and get it done.

But my dad sure did, and he taught me well. I'd do things all the time for him around the house, with no expectation of an allowance. Mowing the lawn and doing other chores was just part of the privilege of having a roof over my head and two loving parents who bought me food, clothes, and all the stuff I needed for school and sports. My dad would give me something to do, and not only would I have to do it, I'd have to do it well.

When I was about 10 years old, my dad introduced me to the concept of working for money. A neighbor of ours had a huge piece of land next to our house that he never did anything with.

He let my dad grow things on his land free of charge, and my dad really took advantage of the opportunity. He grew strawberries, watermelon, corn, squash, and all sorts of other things, and then he'd sell them by the side of the road or at the local farmer's market. I'd be my dad's assistant, and he'd pay me a couple of bucks for helping him out.

As much as I liked making money, and as much as my dad reinforced the idea that work was the way you got ahead in life, he always made sure that my schoolwork and athletics came first. He even set a powerful example for me by never missing a single one of my games or meets in any of the sports I played. That was particularly hard for him because he often had jobs that had him working on shifts. He'd have to swap shifts, and sometimes work double shifts, just to watch me play.

My dad showed me how to be highly productive when I worked, so I could make room in my life for other things that were important to me as a kid. That meant working hard, as well as efficiently. By the time I was about 12 years old, I had friends of mine working for me while I went to baseball practice. I grew strawberries back then, and while I found the time to water everything and pull the weeds, I needed people to help me pick the berries and pack them in little boxes. I'd set a few of my friends up on the job, go to practice, and pay them each a nickel for every box of strawberries they packed when I got back. That experience gave me valuable insights into how to manage people, how to motivate them to work hard, and how to trust them to be accountable. It was also the first time I saw that it was possible to make a profit by helping other people profit at the same time.

My dad was always doing stuff to improve our family's financial position, and he was a big proponent of taking on extra jobs to make extra money. He was a postman during the day. At night, he cleaned bakery floors. On weekends, he'd sell the produce that he grew in our neighbor's field. One of the houses we lived in had an avocado grove in the backyard, and when we lived there he harvested and sold avocados.

Dad was always looking for opportunities to help our family by working harder. His philosophy was simple—as long as you're alive, you might as well do something productive. He never said it quite that way, but that was the gist of it. My dad loved to work, he loved to make money, and he loved his wife and kids. He proved that love each day by working hard and doing the best job he possibly could.

My dad and I got interested in real estate at about the same time. It was actually because of my dad that I got excited about houses. When I was in sixth or seventh grade, my parents started buying and selling homes as a way to get ahead. We'd buy a house, live in it for a couple of years, then sell it so we could trade up to a bigger house in a better part of town. As a postman, my dad learned a lot about property and about which neighborhoods were the best to live in.

I remember being home alone one day when the doorbell rang. I greeted a realtor and a couple who was interested in seeing our house, the one with the avocado grove on the property. I was about 16 years old. The realtor asked if my parents were home and I said no, just me. He appeared disheartened, and he reluctantly asked me if I knew where the property lines were. To his surprise, I replied that I did indeed know where they were, and that I'd be more than happy to show them! I took them all around the property, showed them how the sprinkler valves that irrigated the avocado grove worked, and showed them the whole house inside and out.

I made an impression, and the couple ended up buying the house. The realtor even told my parents that I'd be a pretty good

salesman someday. It was fun, but at age 16 I wasn't really thinking about becoming a real estate tycoon. At that time in my life,
my mind was occupied with thoughts of friends and school, and
I was enjoying both a love and talent for athletics.

By the time I was a teenager, I was beginning to see the importance of a dollar. For the first time in my life, my desires exceeded
my resources. My parents could buy me food, clothes, and the
occasional baseball glove, but they couldn't afford my taste in
cars or dates. I was on my own when it came to wheels, girls, and
other important extras.

I made my dad a proposition. As a boy, I helped my dad pick
oranges on the weekends. He used to pay a guy to let him pick
oranges off his property, and then he'd sell them at a profit. I think
he paid $1 per box and sold them for $3 a box. One day, I asked my
dad if I could run the business on my own. I think he was a little surprised by this takeover attempt, but once again he was impressed
by my initiative. I suspect that he was pretty proud of the fact that
I was becoming a chip off the old block as far as work was concerned, just like when I tore apart his flowerbed as a toddler.

So my dad agreed. He wanted me to succeed, and he felt that
taking over the orange business would be a good experience for
his son. The next weekend, I was on my own, making the princely
sum of about $10 an hour. I was on top of the world and mom and
dad were right there with me, cheering me on.

3

Sports Showed Me How Great It Feels To Win

THE VARSITY BASKETBALL COACH sat my friend Phil Anderson and me down in his office. "Boys, you two are having a great season with the JV team this year."

"Thanks coach," we said. Phil and I were the star sophomores on what was shaping up to be an awesome team. It was early in the season, but we already thought we had a good chance of being CIF League champs that year. Both of us were excited to be part of such a winning team.

"You know that the varsity team isn't doing so great," coach Wetzell said. Truer words could not have been spoken. The varsity team was struggling big-time. They hadn't even won a game yet, which was bad news in a town that lived for high school sporting events.

Phil and I weren't really sure where the coach was going with all this, but then he dropped the bomb. "I'd like to move you boys up to varsity."

Phil and I were speechless and instantly went through a whole flurry of mixed emotions. On the one hand, we were honored to be asked to play at the varsity level as sophomores. High school sports were so huge in Escondido back then, it was kind of like being called up to the pros.

On the other hand, we were already part of a tight team that was having an amazing season and had lots of fan support. It felt great being cheered by the crowd and winning game after game after game. How could we possibly break the team apart and give all that up?

"The team and I could really use your help this year," coach Wetzell pressed.

We struggled with the decision, and finally decided to play at the varsity level. It was exciting to play with the big boys, and our new team-mates treated us with respect.

The fans loved the fact that two sophomores from Orange Glen High were able to compete against the best juniors and seniors from our rivals. The varsity team started doing better, and our varsity victories as sophomores were satisfying, even though we missed the JV team and the JV team missed us.

Organized athletics gave me a chance to shine at school, starting in seventh grade at Orange Glen Elementary School. What I lacked academically, I made up for athletically. When I started playing sports, I acquired an intense competitive spirit and found out that winning gave me a great deal of confidence.

Athletics gave me a reason to keep going to school and even to look forward to it. Because of my athletic ability, I got all kinds of kudos from other students, teachers, coaches, and parents. My picture was in the local newspaper all the time, and I really felt good about myself at a young age.

One day during my junior year of high school, we played a football game against neighboring Fallbrook. Duke Snider, the legendary Dodgers outfielder who was voted into the National Baseball Hall of Fame, lived in Fallbrook and had a son on the opposing team. After the game, Duke Snider came looking for me. He told me how great my game was, and that I had a real future in football. I was a wide receiver, and I made two long touchdown catches on that particular day. Mr. Snider's comment was such an honor and ego boost for a sixteen-year-old, I can't even tell you!

The rewards and accolades I received by participating in sports reinforced my desire to succeed. I was motivated to train hard and play hard. I wasn't much of a spectator, and I didn't spend hours and hours learning professional statistics like some of the other kids did. I just liked to be on the playing field with the chance to beat my opponents.

In elementary school I played football, baseball, and basketball. In high school, most kids picked one favorite sport to play, but I continued to play all three. Whatever season it was, that was my favorite sport.

I wanted all the trophies I could get. I cherished all the ribbons and medals. I relished all the sweet victories. It felt great to win, and I was a winner.

Even today, competition is what life is all about for me. But although I love winning, I'm smart enough to know that I can't win all the time. I believe that losing is okay, as long as you've given 150%. Knowing that you tried your absolute best, it's a lot easier to move on from a loss and hopefully learn something from the experience.

When I was playing sports in school, I had mind-blowing, great games where I was on fire, and other times I couldn't get anything to click. For me, it all comes down to focus. When I look back at the times when I didn't play as well as I could have, it was usually because I was distracted from the task at hand.

It was on the playing field that I really learned that it's better to stay relaxed, calm, and focused. I learned that it was better to see the big picture of the entire game or season than get frustrated or angry about a bungled play, a bad call, or a stupid opponent talking trash. Getting distracted by those things just hurts you in the end. It's not always easy to keep your focus, but this is something I continually try to do in my career because it works the same in business as it does in athletics.

If you have a problem or make a mistake at work, it makes more sense to address it head-on rather than get upset or stew about it for days, weeks, or even longer. Moving through problems quickly and staying focused on the larger goal of winning is a great way to succeed in business.

Except for the one season when I ran track to pass my geometry class, I always played team sports. And even when I was on the track team, one of my best events was the 440 relay—a team event. Playing on teams taught me many valuable lessons that I've applied to my career since the beginning.

The first lesson that's applicable to business is that teams teach you how to get along with people. I met some of my best friends on teams, great guys like Phil Anderson, who played varsity basketball with me in our sophomore year, and Art Duncan, who played football with me and became my first business partner. Art and I are still friends and business partners today, and ours is a rare friendship that many people look for in life but hardly ever find. I can trust Art with anything, and he feels the same about me.

The few close friendships I made while playing sports transcended the teams I was on—these guys were friends with me both on and off the playing field. But more important—as it related to team effectiveness—was the camaraderie I felt with everyone on my teams, whether or not we were friends outside of the sporting experience.

Camaraderie is among the most important elements of effective teams, and it's developed through a team's positive shared experiences. People on teams with a lot of camaraderie celebrate victories, learn from losses, and get psyched up for future challenges together. When there's a lot of camaraderie on a team, the team is definitely greater than the sum of its parts.

I think it's critical for people in a business setting to foster camaraderie as much as possible. I do it all the time through open communication, clearly stated goals that everyone can buy into, words of encouragement, rewards and recognition, and an all-around atmosphere of fun at the office and on the job sites.

The second important business lesson I've learned from team sports is that teams are most effective when each player excels in a specialized role. A group's success depends on everyone doing their individual jobs as best as they can. If a baseball player fails in his role as catcher, pitcher, or first baseman, for example, the entire team could lose the ball game.

The same is true at Michael Crews Development. If my framing crew doesn't put up the underlying structure of a house correctly, then my finishing crew is going to run into problems and the entire house is going to get messed up. This doesn't happen, of course, because we all "work together" by performing our individual tasks with expertise and accountability, so that every other team member can do his or her job as perfectly as possible.

Related to this kind of individual specialization is the third lesson I've learned from team sports. It's the idea that a coach has the responsibility of putting the best people in the right positions. This isn't always a pleasant task, because creating a competitive environment can cause feelings to be hurt. The good news is that the best hard workers thrive on competition, and choosing the best team members is important if you want your business to win.

I want the best people in my company, because I want to beat the other guy. I want my customers to be my biggest fans. If I hire someone just because he's a nice person, or because I feel sorry for him, or for some reason other than how great a contributor he's going to be to the team, then I'm actually letting the whole team down.

Now, I'm well aware of the fact that people often need training to become the best. There'll always be rookies, and it's the manager or leader's responsibility to take raw talent, enthusiasm, and a good work ethic and help people become the best they can be. In this book I talk a lot about a process called upbuilding, which means that while you don't always put the best person in a particular job, you do always build that person up so that he or she becomes the best person for that job.

The fourth and final lesson that I've learned about business from teams is that people on teams really want to perform well for a great coach. I was fortunate to have had great coaches and not-so-great coaches in school. The contrast really made me appreciate how much of a positive impact a great coach can have on a team's success.

When you have a great coach—someone who gives you the skills and tools you need to succeed, someone who encourages you and publicly rewards your achievements—you really, really want to perform. I mean, you really want to go all out and do some amazing things for them. A great business leader, like a great coach, inspires the members of his or her team to work harder and dig deeper than they ever thought they could, in order to make it possible for everyone on the team to enjoy the thrill of victory.

Victory is such an incredible feeling—and such an important requirement for success—that I make it a point to apply the lessons I've learned about winning sports teams to create winning business teams every single day.

The people at the highest levels of management in my company, for example, are members of what we call the Development Team. These people are highly specialized players who I consider to be the best at what they do. My top contractors make up the A-Team. These skilled craftspeople aren't my employees, but their performance is critical to the success of Michael Crews Development.

Using team terminology reinforces the idea that all of us are working together to win. And it spreads through the entire organization. Each of my Development Team and A-Team members leads another team of people who focus on a particular area of building and selling houses. And every person on these specialized teams is also an integral part of the larger company team.

Here are just some of the specific ways I apply the four lessons I've learned about teambuilding to my business:

Lesson One—Build Camaraderie: The Development Team meets as a group once a week to make sure we're on track toward meeting our annual sales goals, which are publicly stated throughout the company on T-shirts, hats, and signs. The Development Team goes out to dinner at least once a quarter, and I've taken Development Team and A-Team members on trips to Tahiti and the Caribbean. We often host spontaneous lunches and activities for different crews, and we host an annual Christmas party for everyone in the company. Plus, every day we try to have fun and not take ourselves too seriously.

Lesson Two—Define Roles: Michael Crews Development is set up differently than most other development companies. Everyone in the company touches every one of our projects, so every person's job is highly dependent on somebody else's job. When building a house, somebody is always literally covering up somebody else's work, so it's extremely important for people to do their best, to be accountable for any mistakes they might make, and to be outspoken about any problems they discover.

Lesson Three—Find The Best People: The fact that our business is successful helps us attract the best and the brightest, because people who like to win like to be part of a winning team. I also help all of my co-workers reach their full potential by upbuilding them and encouraging them to upbuild themselves (more on this in chapter 12). The camaraderie we have at Michael Crews Development makes people stay on our team a lot longer than they do at some other companies. Long-term employees are critical for sustained success and for helping new employees get up to speed as efficiently as possible.

Lesson Four—Be The Best Coach: With the best people in place, it's my job to motivate my team members to work hard, give them confidence in their abilities, show them how much I value their contributions, create camaraderie, foster accountability, and give them whatever else they need to succeed—from advice and material resources to encouraging words and rewards for achievement. My team members also need to know they can talk to me about anything without upsetting me, and I need to trust that they're always giving 150% for the greater good of the business.

It amazes me when business leaders don't follow the tried-and-true model for business success that comes from the playing field. It amazes me when business leaders don't take the time to build camaraderie, when it can make a team greater than the sum of its parts. It amazes me when business leaders don't find the best people to perform very specialized functions so that their people can take pride in a single area of expertise and benefit the entire business. And it amazes me when business leaders can be bad coaches when the rewards of being a great coach are so tremendous.

Organized sports showed me how great it feels to win, but it also made me face a harsh reality. As I progressed through high school, I dreamed about a career as a professional athlete. For a long time, I really believed that I was going to become a professional basketball player. My intention was to go to college and focus on basketball, which I thought was my best sport. But after I graduated from high school, I had the chance to play summer ball for Palomar College.

As good as I was, the college guys I was playing against were playing on a whole different level. And as much as I didn't want to admit it, they were better than me. They were a lot better than me.

It was then that I realized that I wasn't the best person for the job, and that I probably wouldn't be able to build myself up to the level that would allow me to make it to the NBA. This realization hit me pretty hard, and I remember making the conscious decision to give up my quest to become a pro athlete. I remember it like it was yesterday.

Fortunately, I was able to find something I was good at, focus on it, and apply what I learned from a very satisfying high school athletic career to the field of business.

4

How I Built A Career
That Generates Millions

I WAS REALLY NERVOUS before I entered Knox Williams's office on that summer day in 1975. Mr. Williams was my first full-time boss, and I had to tell him that I was leaving the company. I was 19 years old.

His office was impressive, complete with the big wooden desk, oversized chair, and two leather client chairs. It was always a little intimidating for me to go into his office, and on that day I was scared.

"Mr. Williams," I began. "I'm giving you my two-week notice. I've decided to go into real estate."

There was a long silence.

"No, Mike, you can't do that," he finally said.

I thought he might be upset, but I wasn't expecting this.

"I have to, Mr. Williams. I got my real estate license and everything."

"You can't do it."

"With all due respect, sir, my mind's made up."

"There's no way I'm letting you leave here."

At this point, I was getting anxious.

"Why not?!"

"Because I could never replace you, Mike."

I knew then that he was just trying to show me how much he valued the hard work I had given him for the past year and a half. It was his humorous way of showing me how much he appreciated my service to his company. Boy, was I relieved when I realized that he wasn't being serious.

"Mike, I had to leave an employer to start my own business," he said. "I understand what you're going through, and I knew I wasn't going to be able to keep you around here forever. You're the best employee we've ever had. I thank you for that, Mike, and I wish you all the best."

———————

After high school, I knew that I wasn't going to be a famous ballplayer. But I wanted to keep winning in life. Ever since my first Little League game, competing and winning has been a big thrill for me—and I don't see that changing anytime soon.

Graduating from high school was difficult for me on one level, because it meant that I could no longer draw strength or joy from competitive athletics. I didn't want the victories to end. As great as my high school years were, I certainly didn't want my contributions to the Orange Glen High School baseball, basketball, football, and track teams to be the highlight of my entire life.

So on another level, graduating from high school was exciting. I had a whole big future to look forward to. And after I realized that college wasn't going to be a productive way to spend the next four years of my life, I decided that I had better do something I was good at—work.

At the time, I was working part time at a 7-Eleven store for $1.65 an hour, but that didn't discourage me or keep me from dreaming big. I knew that if I worked hard, stayed patient and focused, and looked for opportunities, I could make great things happen for myself.

Every day, I'd look through the newspaper for full-time employment. One day, an ad that said "Route Sales" caught my eye. I had no idea what it was all about, but it had the word "sales" in it and that was good enough for me. Ever since the realtor who sold our house when I was 16 years old told my parents that I'd be a good salesman someday, the idea of a career in sales was always in the back of my mind.

I responded to the ad and began my relationship with Knox Williams. He was a small guy, full of fire and energy. He was a real dynamo and I learned a lot from him. He gave me my first full-time job as a driver for the Rayne Water Conditioning Company, a soft water service. He had the franchise for North San Diego County (locally referred to simply as North County), which covers the towns of Bonsall, Carlsbad, Del Mar, Escondido, Fallbrook, La Costa, Oceanside, Pala, Pauma Valley, Poway, Ramona, Rancho Bernardo, Rancho Santa Fe, San Luis Rey, San Marcos, Solana Beach, Valley Center, and Vista.

Knox Williams mostly hired drivers who were young and strong, and as an 18-year-old jock with pretty good size, I fit the bill. It was my job to deliver and install refill tanks for customers who lived along one of the four or five routes the company had.

The tanks were big silver things, filled with resin that filtered calcium and magnesium out of the water. They were incredibly heavy—they weighed 85, 115, and 160 pounds, depending on the size of the tank—and I used to carry them on my shoulders. I remember walking up driveways with these huge tanks on my back while little dogs nipped at my ankles. We were supposed to roll the biggest tanks on a dolly, but sometimes it was harder to lift the tanks on and off the dolly than it was to just carry them all the way from the truck to the customer's house. It was tough, physical work, and it only paid $2.80 an hour.

An hourly wage of $2.80 times eight hours, times five days, times 52 weeks equals $5,824.00 a year. I wasn't great at math, but I was good enough to know that I wasn't going to get very far on that kind of salary, even back in the mid 1970s.

But I learned from my dad that a great way to get ahead is to find ways to do extra work. I got a job delivering the *Los Angeles Times* that started at two o'clock each morning, and I kept my thriving fruit and vegetable business going on the weekends.

And even at the water company, I looked for opportunities. Mr. Williams told all of the delivery guys that we could make extra money if we signed up new customers. It was strictly voluntary—commission only—and we had to do it on our own time.

I told Mr. Williams that I was interested, so after about a week on my delivery route he took me out one Saturday and we canvassed door-to-door. That day, Knox Williams reinforced a lot of the things I already suspected about sales. His philosophy, like mine, is that you don't need to have a hard-sell approach. Selling is strictly a numbers game, which means you just have to get your message out to the people who want to receive it. We made a sale that day to a woman who told us that she was waiting for us. She had wanted soft water for a long time, but had never gotten around to calling anyone. We rang the right doorbell at the right time.

But we also met with some objections, and Knox showed me how adept he was at handling them. If someone complained about price, he never got upset or defensive. He'd simply ask if he could demonstrate how purchasing the service would actually save the customer money. If someone said they didn't know anything about the service we were offering, Knox would politely offer to explain the benefits and show them how it would be to their advantage to place an order. Knox was really passionate about soft water. He knew everything about it, and he was able to quickly and clearly articulate its benefits with sincerity. He really believed—and still does to this day—in the positive impact that soft water can have on the American household.

I had fun that Saturday, and Knox had confidence in me. He let me go on my own, and I started working hard to make sales right away. While I was on my route during the week, I'd leave notes for people in the neighborhood. "Hi, this is Mike from Rayne Water Conditioning," I'd write. "I'll be back in the neighborhood on Saturday and would like to tell you about our service." I'd also leave behind a brochure and a free notepad that had the company's logo on it.

When Saturday rolled around, I'd go back to the houses where I left notes. If someone was home, I'd be able to break the ice with, "Hi, I'm Mike from Rayne Water Conditioning. I'm glad I caught you today—did you get the notepad I left you?" It was easy for me to talk to people, and even if I didn't make a sale, I'd at least have a pleasant conversation that could possibly lead to a sale or a referral at another time.

I could normally make about three sales each Saturday and earn as much as $50, which wasn't bad for a day's work back then. If people weren't home, I'd leave more notes. I kept a notebook with me so I could keep track of the people I contacted and the people I needed to call on again.

The opportunity was there for all the delivery guys to make extra money, but I was the only one taking advantage of it. The other drivers all thought I was stupid to give up my Saturdays, but I thought I was smart to gain the extra income and experience. It seemed to be working for me, because every month I was the top salesperson at the company.

One day, I asked Knox if he had any information about customers who had canceled their service with the water company. I figured that it would be pretty easy to convince former customers to sign up for the service again. Maybe they missed having the soft water but hadn't gotten around to calling us, like the lady Knox and I made our first sale to. Maybe our former customers were making more money now and could afford the service again. Or maybe they had cooled off after a perceived customer service problem.

Still another possibility was that a former customer had moved away and someone else was living in his or her house. Because we left all the plumbing in place after a cancellation and just took back our tank, I could offer free installation to people who lived in houses that were already outfitted for our service.

Knox gave me all the information I needed to succeed (he was a great boss!) and we made a deal. I'd get a commission for every customer I could bring back to the company, in addition to getting commissions for all the new customers I signed up.

I sold my heart out and did pretty well at it, even though I had my share of doors slammed in my face. But I took it all in stride, and never took rejection personally or got mad. The people who ultimately said no to me just didn't want the water service, and all I really needed to do was find the people who did want it.

Selling was like a game or a competition to me, and I was motivated to win. I was constantly looking for creative ways to expand my territory. One of the best ideas I had was to approach people who had just moved into new housing developments—a soft water conditioner was perfect for a brand-new home!

No one was going to work harder than I was. I loved working then, as I do now, because I saw it as the way I was able to win at the game of life. Opportunities are all around us, and sometimes it's as simple as getting off your butt if you want to take advantage of them.

The sales part of my job was a lot of fun, but the delivery part of the job was taking its toll on me. Carrying tanks all day brought me to the doctor's office on more than one occasion. My back was killing me from carrying those heavy tanks, and the doctor told me that if I stayed in that job I'd have an awfully short career. After 18 months with the water company, I realized that I had to do something different.

One day, I was having lunch underneath a tree, and I opened up the newspaper to look for a new job. An ad caught my eye that said "Real Estate Class Starting." The ad also said that it would only take two weeks to get a real estate license.

I said to myself, "I'm going to do that."

After all, I had some experience—I helped sell my parents' house when I was 16 years old. Plus, it dawned on me that selling houses could actually be a career with some longevity. Everyone needs to live in a house, and I wouldn't have to lift them up and carry them around while little dogs nipped at my ankles.

So I went to real estate school, and found out that I had to take a test to get my license. Since I don't read well that was really bad news for me. But I figured that if I could memorize the right answers to all the questions that were going to be on the test, I'd be able to pass.

It was kind of like the way I got through the multiplication tables in third grade. I focused really hard on memorizing all the right answers—I didn't waste my time on the wrong ones—and sure enough, I passed the test and got my license.

Even before I had proof from the State of California that I was able to sell houses, I started looking for a company to work for. Lots of the smaller companies said they'd hire me when I got my license, but I received a far different response from the Forest E. Olson (a regional chain that would later be bought out by Coldwell Banker) office in Escondido.

The manager of that office laughed at me.

"How old are you, kid?" he asked.

"Nineteen."

"You're too young to sell houses!" Grant Olson (no relation to Forest) headed up one of the most successful real estate offices in North County. "People have to trust you with their life savings," Mr. Olson said. "Why in the world would they listen to some kid who didn't even go to college?"

Now it was a challenge. I wanted more than anything to be a part of this office, but I had to prove to them that I was serious. I kept stopping by with questions and status reports, looking for ways to improve my chances of getting hired.

"You've got the wrong kind of car," Mr. Olson told me one time when I was visiting the office.

"What kind of car does a realtor drive?" I asked.

"A four-door car, son," he said with a chuckle. "It's easier for your clients when you're driving them around." I'm sure he must have thought I was crazy, and thought that would be the end of it.

A few days later, I returned with a four-door, white Chevy Nova.

"What do you think, Mr. Olson?"

I kept persisting, but they kept turning me down. They never heard of a teenager selling houses before. But after three or four interviews, Mr. Olson agreed to give me a chance. That's all I wanted, because I knew I'd do a great job.

"Thank you Mr. Olson. You won't regret it."

I wanted to work there so badly, and it was a thrill to be finally hired on. I was planning to keep all my extra jobs, but Mr. Olson had a different idea. He told me to stop everything else and put 150% of my energy into real estate. This would soon prove to be great advice.

When I first started working at Forest E. Olson, they put me in what they called the Fast Start Program. For two weeks, a group of us new realtors heard lectures from sales trainers, acted out skits in which we played the roles of realtors and buyers, and did other exercises to get motivated to sell houses. I ate these classes up and took full advantage of them. By the time the program was over, I felt like I was ready to conquer the world!

I wanted to hit the ground running and prove myself right away, and I set my sights high from the start. The Forest E. Olson offices in our area offered what they called a Quota Buster Award for top-performing realtors. It was an honor to receive this distinction, because it had to be earned. Any agent could get it, but a lot of hard work was required—you had to complete seven or more transactions in a calendar month.

Every agent wanted that award, and the promise of receiving it made some of us work as hard as we possibly could—especially me. Completing seven transactions in a month was pretty challenging. The average agent probably completed two or three transactions in a month, so getting to seven was something of a stretch. Even the best agents only got the Quota Buster Award once or twice a year.

But there was an amazing guy in a nearby office named Tommy Hopkins. He would later go on to national fame as a motivational real estate sales trainer, but at that time he was one of the hottest agents in the area. He held the record for the most consecutive Quota Buster Awards received—10 in a row.

From day one I set out to beat that record, and right off the bat I got the Quota Buster Award during my first month in business. Mr. Olson and the rest of the people in the office thought it was just beginner's luck. But then I kept getting the Quota Buster Award, and the people in the office were beginning to see how hard I was working. As the months went by, people started expecting me to get the award.

I got the Quota Buster Award for the first eleven months I was in the real estate business. Every single month—and they told me I was too young to sell houses! I beat Tommy Hopkins's record, but, I have to tell you, the month my streak ended was devastating. I never wanted that streak to end.

I soon got over it, however, because in addition to getting the Quota Buster Award, I was also making money. I was so busy selling real estate, I didn't even have time to cash my commission checks. I just kept the checks in a drawer, and whenever I needed some money I'd go cash one. Each commission check was only a few hundred bucks, but they really added up. I was earning about $50,000 a year as a realtor, up from the $6,000 salary I was making at the water company.

I loved selling houses, and I loved having money flow in. I was driven to succeed. I worked on real estate twelve hours a day, six or seven days a week. I called up all my old friends from high school to see if they wanted to buy houses. When they told me they couldn't afford it, I suggested that they go in on a deal with a friend or two—owning a house was better than renting an apartment, and they could sell the house in a few years and make a profit. I put lots of my friends in their first houses, and they spread the word to other friends, who told even more friends. On and on and on it went.

I enjoyed helping people get into their first houses, and I became sort of a specialist for first-time home buyers. Everything just snowballed, and I kept getting referred to more and more people who wanted to get into their first house. It's amazing, but it really works: When you're honest with people and sincere in your efforts to help them, you get a lot more back in return.

The word of mouth that my services generated was tremendous, but I didn't let my guard down. In addition to working and expanding my personal network, I spent a lot of time involved in a tedious but valuable activity we called farming. If I sold a house in a particular neighborhood, or if I had a buyer who wanted a house in a certain area, I'd get out the big reverse directory (a comprehensive listing of property addresses and corresponding phone numbers) and start cold-calling every house in the vicinity.

When someone answered the phone, I'd introduce myself and say that I had a client who wanted to buy a house in his or her neighborhood.

"Would you be interested in selling your house?" I'd ask.

If they didn't answer the phone, I'd go ring their doorbell. If they still weren't home, I'd leave behind pens, pencils, golf balls—whatever I had with my name on it—and a note saying that I could sell their house for them if they were interested. I was relentless in tracking people down. If I could talk to them and they decided to work with me, I became the listing broker for their property.

I learned early on that it was a huge advantage to be the listing broker on a house that was up for sale. Listing brokers were guaranteed to get a commission when their houses sold, and they had the help of all the other agents in town showing the house to prospective buyers. The more listings I got, the more people I'd have helping me sell my houses, and the more productive and profitable my business would be.

It dawned on me that a team of hard workers could be more effective than a single hard worker. I always knew that I could get ahead by working hard, and throughout my career I realized more and more that I could get even further with the help of other hard workers.

As smart as I thought I was about trying to be the listing agent as often as possible, it took me two years before I figured out what was really going on in the real estate office. I was making great money for a 21-year-old, but the office manager was doing better than anybody. The office manager was making money on every single house that was sold through the office— because he had all the agents in the office working for him.

So I said to myself, "Okay, I'm going to be a manager and make a lot of money."

This was another example of always looking for opportunities to improve my situation and enlist the assistance of other hard workers. I could have gone along selling houses for the rest of my career and I would have done pretty well in life, but I wanted to keep challenging myself and compete at higher levels.

Mr. Olson had been promoted, and by that time I was reporting to a man by the name of Hugh Justice. I went into his office and told him that I wanted to be in management.

History repeated itself.

"You're only 21 years old, Mike—you can't manage a real estate office," he said. "Wait until you're 40 or 50."

Hadn't he learned anything from my past experiences?

"If that's how you feel about it, Mr. Justice, I think I'm going to have to quit working here."

Mr. Justice knew how well I was doing for the company (and for him), so he asked me not to leave.

"Just hang in there a little while longer, Michael," he said. "We'll try to figure something out for you."

His promise made me cool down a little, and I sold houses for another 45 days. Then Mr. Justice called me into his office and announced that if I wanted to be in management, I had to take a management test. He told me it was going to be tough, and that I shouldn't expect to do very well on it without a college education.

Well, that was all the motivation I needed to prove him wrong. I studied harder for that test than I'd ever studied for anything in my life, and I passed it with flying colors. Mr. Justice and the rest of the management team couldn't believe it. The test results didn't lie, but my bosses were still against hiring such a young manager. So they cooked up another plan to get me to fail.

The manager of the Poway office was going on vacation and they asked me to fill in for two weeks. It was a terrible office, down to only 12 realtors from a capacity of 35. I got there and all I saw were the empty desks. It was depressing, and the 12 people who remained in the office were pretty beaten down and discouraged.

So I just started kicking butt—and the realtors in the Poway office started to get excited about selling houses again. I did everything I could to help them, and we were quickly becoming something of a team. My bosses took notice after my first week, and they called me up and said, "Don't move, just keep doing what you're doing. The guy who had that office won't be coming back from vacation."

The Poway office was mine, and I made it my mission to turn the place around. I got my agents together, and we formulated office plans and goals. I told them what I expected from them and how I would help them succeed, and we came up with an office slogan, "Do It Together In Poway!"

In 12 months, I rebuilt that office to 38 agents. We were over capacity and I actually had people sharing desks. There were two or three extra people, and whoever had the fewest sales each month had to share a desk. It was a friendly competition, but all of the agents had to earn their right to their own desks. And that meant that everybody in the office was going to sell more houses.

To turn this office around so fast, I built camaraderie like there was no tomorrow. I did it by helping people get their jobs done.

If an agent had a listing appointment, then—boom!—I was right there with them. If a gal had a late-night property showing and was nervous about it, I'd go with her to make her feel safe. I did everything I could to proactively help my agents close their sales. The managers in my old office never left their desks.

My interactive coaching/managing style really made a difference, and my agents wanted to perform. They appreciated the help they got from their manager, and in return they got results for me. Together, we created a tight and enthusiastic team that had fun, kept the lines of communication wide open, and worked hard to sell a lot of houses.

I became a better manager, because I got involved with the people I was in charge of managing. I wasn't afraid to go right into the trenches with them if that's what it took. They knew that I was once in their shoes as a regular agent, so they knew I could understand any problems they were having. Some managers, in any profession, seem to forget what it took to get them to their management positions, and that just doesn't make sense to me. It was my role to upbuild my agents and help them close as many sales as possible, and my arsenal was filled with my personal experiences of selling houses on my own.

In addition to hard work, I encouraged "hard play" to help my agents stay motivated and add life and energy to the once-dreary office. We had a beach party every few months, I took the team to the ball game sometimes if we met our monthly listing and commission goals, I offered prizes for top performers like trips for two to Las Vegas, and I published agent birthdays in our monthly office newsletter.

One day, when we were up to about 25 agents, we all had to go to another office in Claremont for a joint meeting. We were always referred to as "the hicks from the hills" because Poway was so rural, so I decided to play into that perception and liven up what would otherwise be a boring meeting.

All of us "hicks" from Poway walked into the Claremont office wearing overalls and straw hats. We threw hay all over their office and talked in our best hillbilly accents. I think we shocked the folks in Claremont at first, but they got a big kick out of the show. And all of us from the Poway office left the meeting feeling great. We were unified in a terrific team effort that helped us all get better at selling houses, even though it had nothing to do with selling houses.

Fun things do a lot to boost morale and create an atmosphere where people want to help each other succeed. The things we were doing "together in Poway" created a buzz in North County's real estate world, and more and more agents wanted to join our winning team. It seemed as though everyone wanted to work for the wild young manager who was reenergizing the office in Poway.

After my first year on the job, one of the guys on my team named Lee Apple put together this poem about me:

> You should see old Mike on the tennis court
> He can hardly hit the ball.
> The way he flails his arms and legs
> Reminds you of urban sprawl!
>
> He became our boss a year ago
> At the age of twenty-three.
> We asked, "Has F.E.O. gone mad?"
> This guy's still in puberty!
>
> With his big blue eyes, his curly hair,
> His cheeks still covered with fuzz,
> Who'd ever think that he'd be the one
> Who'd make this place really buzz?

That funny poem was part of a surprise the whole team planned to wish me a happy birthday. We were in our weekly Thursday morning meeting when I noticed a very attractive girl in a tennis outfit walk into the room. She came all the way up to my nose and said, "Hi, I'm Melissa. I've just been hired to be your private tennis instructor." My team all pitched in to get me tennis lessons and presented them to me in a creative way.

This was typical of the kind of fun and camaraderie we developed in the Poway office. They were exciting times for everyone involved, and even today I get calls and greetings from people who worked with me back then. Working hard allowed me to do a few small things to touch their lives, and the rewards are still coming back to me.

After about two years of upbuilding this struggling office to the point where it was rolling in money, I petitioned my bosses for a district manager's job. That would have put me in charge of 15 offices.

No surprise, it was the same thing all over again.

"You're only 24 years old and you've never been to college. You can't be a district manager."

This time, I put my business cards down on my boss's desk and quit my association with Forest E. Olson. My supervisors accepted my resignation, but they told me that they were going to hang on to my cards. They "knew" that I'd never make it on my own and that eventually I'd come crawling back to them, begging for my old job back. They told me that I'd never be able to start my own company.

I walked out of the office, determined to make it on my own. I often wonder if they still have those business cards!

I never looked back, because I was ready to take myself to the next level. I was ready for a new challenge, a new game, a new competition.

In the spring of 1980, I opened up MDC Real Estate Investments. MDC stood for Michael David Crews. I figured that putting my name on the door would hold me more accountable to my customers and motivate me to succeed even more. Plus, I had a lot of equity built up in my name. In my particular slice of America, people knew who I was because they had seen my name on hundreds of real estate signs and knew about my reputation for selling houses.

Instead of just selling houses, however, I wanted to build them. I wasn't sure how to do it, but I was eager to figure it out. Let me tell you, learning by doing is part of the fun in life. However, be careful that you temper your enthusiasm and start smaller than you think—or "know"—you should. If you're learning a new skill or starting your own business, heeding this advice will help you minimize the impact of mistakes and prevent you from getting in too deep if things don't go as well as you'd like them to. It'll also give you enough reserve energy to regroup and keep trying again if things don't work out in the beginning.

When I was first on my own, I noticed a house that was on the market for awhile. It was on the corner of a really bad intersection, and the seller was asking $70,000—which was about $5,000 more than it was really worth.

When I looked at the house, however, I believed that there might be an opportunity there to do something different. I noticed that the house was built all the way on one side of the property and had a giant side yard. I thought that was kind of interesting, so I did some investigating. I went to city hall in Escondido and talked to some people about what zoning meant. I found out that I could make two legal lots out of the property and put another house on the second lot. The beauty of the plan was that I'd basically be getting the land for the second house for free.

I paid full price for the $70,000 house, which was all of a sudden a great bargain.

After I got the house, I looked in the phone book to find an engineer who could help me split the lot. Mike Wunderlin (who, by the way, still works with me today) was just starting his own business, too. I hired him and we worked hard to figure out the best way to divide the property to accommodate another house. He did all the drawings, and I ran around to get approvals from the city. It took us about six months to get a line drawn on a piece of paper, but we did it the right way and I learned an awful lot about working with the local government. It didn't hurt to make a few friends at city hall.

Now all I needed was a second house to put on the lot. I was thinking about building something, but before I could even start figuring out the details an interesting opportunity presented itself. I noticed in the very back of the newspaper that the City of Escondido was auctioning off a house that had to be moved from its current location.

Before the auction date, I went to the house and looked at it. I thought to myself, "Well, that's a house alright!"

It wasn't anything spectacular, but at least when I walked inside everything looked pretty normal. And fortunately, it wasn't very big. I decided that I could probably figure out how to pick up the house and move it, and that it would probably be cheaper to do that than build a new house from scratch.

So I went to the auction—I got there early because I'm always on time. I had a blank check with me, and I had no idea what was going to happen. I sat down and waited, expecting more and more people to show up as it got closer to the appointed time.

No one came.

I was the only person sitting in the courtroom when the judge walked in from his chambers. He sat down at his bench, we acknowledged each other, and we sat quietly for what seemed like forever.

After a few minutes, the judge stood up and said, "How much are you going to give me for this house?"

I looked around the room and said, "Your Honor, there's nobody here."

"You're here," he replied. "How much are you going to pay for the house?"

"I don't know," was all I could come up with. I had imagined that there'd be a big crowd of people there, all wanting this house. I thought that someone would start the bidding at a certain price, and that I'd fight as hard as I could to get the property until I either got it or the price got too high for me.

The judge finally said, "I need to know how much you're going to pay for the house."

I was kind of scared at this point and didn't really know what to say. "How about 500 bucks?" is what came out of my mouth.

The judge raised his gavel and slammed it down. The sound reverberated through the empty courtroom and the judge shouted, "Sold!"

"I just bought a house," was all I could think to myself.

I was kind of numb and excited at the same time. I gave the judge a check for $500, and he told me that I had 30 days to get the house off the property.

"I just bought a house."

At that point, I didn't even really know for sure if the house was going to fit on my lot. I thought it would, but now that I owned it, I was in a bit of a panic. I called Mike Wunderlin for some reassurance. He told me that of course, the house would fit, and he even suggested some ways I could place it on the property once I got it there. That was a huge relief, but there was still the minor little detail of getting the house from where it sat to where I wanted it, about three miles away.

It was ironic that I entered the world of real estate in order to stop picking up water tanks, and now I had to figure out how to pick up an entire house.

At that time Art Duncan, my football buddy from high school, was building houses with his dad. I decided to give him a call and see if he had any ideas about how I could move the house and secure it on my lot.

"I've never moved a house before," he said.

I made him an offer. "I'll give you a 50% interest in the house if you help me figure out how to get it where I need it to go, and then help me fix it up."

He thought I was crazy, but he agreed. His dad thought we were both insane. We laid a foundation on my lot and paid a house mover $15,000 to move the house. We secured the house on the property, remodeled it, and cleaned it all up. We put in the plumbing, a driveway, and all the electrical work. We probably spent another $15,000 to get the house in market condition, bringing the total investment to about $30,000.

Soon, I sold the house to a friend for $67,000 and split the profits with Art, fifty-fifty.

This was truly one of the great experiences of my life. It felt risky, exciting, fun, crazy, and challenging, but it also seemed well within the realm of possibility. It was certainly an unusual thing to do—Channel 8 News even came out and did a story about us— and the fact that it all actually worked out helped to cement a friendship and give me more evidence that hard work can pay off.

After our first taste of success, Art and I decided to go into business together. We gave birth to Duncan/Crews Development in 1981.

Our next few projects pretty much followed the same model as our first one, except for the fact that we started building houses of our own. I'd look for existing houses with enough land to legally add one or two more units, and then we'd put up new construction next to the existing houses. With projects as small as we were doing, it made a huge difference in terms of our profitability to be able to get "free land" for the new houses we were building.

Art and his cousin Mark Duncan (who also still works with me today) came up with a few simple floor plans for 1,000–1,500 square-foot starter homes, and we built them all ourselves. Art had the building experience, so he led the construction side of the business.

It was my responsibility to find the land, get all the paper-work taken care of, and sell the houses. When I wasn't busy, I'd help Art as much as possible, and I learned a lot about building myself—not by watching it being done, but by actually getting in there and doing the job.

Art and I often worked together side-by-side, high up on a house, hammering nails. There was nothing I wouldn't or couldn't do. Art would ask me to help pour foundations, and I'd help pour foundations. He'd ask me to frame houses, and I'd frame houses. I was always willing to jump in the ditch and help lay sewer, electrical, and water lines. We put up drywall, painted, installed appliances, and did just about everything else ourselves. It was actually pretty easy to figure everything out, but it was definitely hard work!

While we were building relatively simple starter homes for young people, we always wanted to build the best houses we could and sell them at affordable prices. With this mindset, we had to be creative. One of the things we wanted to do was put on tile roofs instead of the cheaper composite shingle roofs that most of our competitors were using. To do this, we used our small vol-ume to our advantage and purchased seconds from the tile fac-tory. This allowed us to offer a much better roof for a much lower price. We were also able to put in attractive fences and landscap-ing in the front yards, which made Duncan/Crews houses a lot more attractive to first-time home buyers. People took notice and saw that they were getting a better value with our product, and we were creating demand for future projects with every house we sold.

It was a major turn-on for us when a young family moved into one of our houses and told us how happy they were. It was one of the rewards of our hard work that we didn't even expect, and it made all the effort that we put into building and selling our houses even more worthwhile. I had a similar feeling when I was working at Forest E. Olson and helped people get into their first houses, but it was nothing like the satisfaction I got when it was a house I had built with my own hands.

As Art and I perfected our product, and as we perfected our system of building one or two small houses on small, improved lots, we eventually became eager to see if we could take what we had learned and apply it on a larger scale. With increased confidence in our abilities and an increased demand for our houses, we started putting five or more houses on a single piece of land. We were now getting into official subdivision territory.

Our first really big deal was a 10-unit project we called Mill-brook Park. It was the first project we did that had a name. The rule is that anything over five houses can be classified as a subdivision, allowing you to name the project and any roads you build inside it.

Builders often use the geographical and topographical influences of the land to come up with names for their subdivisions, but I've even named some of our developments after my kids. Drive around Valley Center, California and you'll see Ashley Park, Tyler Peak, Justin Ranch, and Sky Ridge. (We'll have to see what we come up with for my newborn son, Jet!) We've even auctioned off the chance to name projects and streets to help raise money for the local Boys & Girls Clubs. I still remember how happy one little girl was about a development called McKenna Heights, all because her parents had won the opportunity to name it after her.

When we broke ground on Millbrook Park in 1987—six years after starting our business—Art and I were scared. We had never done 10 houses before, and we weren't even planning to do it then. I had found a great piece of land that could accommodate five houses, and we were simply going to move ahead with another five-unit project. The city, however, told us that if we wanted to develop the property, we'd have to put what's known as a knuckle in the road we had to build.

A knuckle is simply a turn, but it's a lot more expensive to build a road with a knuckle in it than it is to build a road without one. Even I could figure out that geometry problem. We were hoping to build a straight road, but the city wanted the turn built so that, in the future, it would be easier to connect our property to an adjoining piece of undeveloped land.

To make the project economically viable, we needed to obtain both properties and develop them at the same time ourselves. I contacted the owners of the second piece of land and asked them if they were interested in selling. They were.

This was good news for us, but it also meant that we had to borrow more money and extend ourselves farther than we ever had before. To protect ourselves, we thought the project through, making sure we had an exit strategy that would at least allow us to break even, and we methodically managed the project like we did all of the smaller ones we had done previously. It worked out really, really well.

By this time in our careers, the banks were starting to believe in us. We always made it a priority to pay the banks off first—before we took any profit—and they appreciated this. Many people think that banks want people to take as long as possible to pay off their loans because of the interest, but the truth is that banks make more of a profit on the upfront fees. When banks get their money back sooner, they can make new loans and get more upfront cash.

Because we relied on banks to finance our development projects, it made sense for us to work hard at developing strong relationships with the bankers in our vicinity from the very beginning. Paying the banks back first wasn't always easy, but the practice served us well as the scale of our projects grew.

I remember one particularly tough time when I was working by myself on a project called Silver Oaks. Back then, North County was experiencing the worst economic time in its history. Nobody was building houses, because nobody was buying houses. Interest rates were as high as 18%.

But at that time I was already committed to Silver Oaks, and I had to build it out in order for my company to stay whole. I gave the go-ahead to start grading, and soon after that we started building. Other developers thought I was crazy, and some of my fiercest competitors were hoping that my "stupid" decision would shut me down for good. I didn't make much money on Silver Oaks, but in reality it was the launching pad for tremendous growth in my career. I was able to pay the banks, and from then on they trusted me completely.

I'm jumping ahead here a little bit, but the point of this story is important because it's a lesson in what really matters most in business—integrity. By laying down a foundation of trust and honesty with the banks, it didn't matter so much to them that my projects made sense, it mattered more that the people involved in my projects made sense. This didn't happen overnight. It was a gradual, step-by-step process that involved a lot of hard work to consistently pay back loans before I even paid myself. I can borrow millions of dollars today with no questions asked if I want to, but I'd never be able to do it if Art and I hadn't paid back the first $50,000 we borrowed more than two decades ago.

With the banks behind us after our Millbrook Park deal, Art and I were able to tackle bigger and bigger projects. Before too long, we were starting to build entire neighborhoods instead of just little groups of houses. But as impressive as 50-unit or 100-unit subdivisions may seem, both are basically built the same way a single house is built. Mastering the details involved in building our smaller projects made it a lot easier to figure out how to build more extensive ones. It gave us a lot of extra energy to focus on the new details we had to master, like procuring more materials, learning new city regulations, and managing more people.

Everything went relatively smoothly for Art and me because we were so patient when it came to growing the company. We never took on a project that we thought we couldn't handle. We had our share of problems, but we knew in the long run that we'd have many more successes than failures if we mastered the details of what we were doing and took on bigger projects only when we felt ready.

Sometimes, however, our best planning and strategic thinking couldn't prepare us for the unexpected. Art and I got into our first real pickle when we were working on a 45-unit subdivision called Orange Glen Estates and a 50-unit subdivision called Hidden Valley Homes. Hidden Valley Homes was being developed on a piece of land on Washington Street in Escondido that we bought for $500,000, and Orange Glen Estates was going to go on land we purchased out of foreclosure for $900,000.

The Hidden Valley Homes deal was complete, and Orange Glen Estates was in escrow when another really beautiful property on Washington Street became available. Located right next to our Hidden Valley Homes site, it could accommodate 30 houses and was being sold for $1 million by the comedians, Cheech and Chong.

This property was just too good to pass up, and Art and I wanted to make a deal as quickly as possible. I remember going to Los Angeles for a meeting with Cheech and Chong's lawyers on the 40th floor of a big office building downtown. There we were in this big, dark conference room lined from floor to ceiling with law books. Three high-powered attorneys surrounded the big conference table. We didn't know what was going to happen.

After a few minutes that seemed like forever, Cheech walked into the room (at least I'm pretty sure it was Cheech). He walked over to the head lawyer, looked over at us, leaned over to the attorney, and said in a heavily-accented whisper for all to hear, "These guys got the money?" That broke the ice and we soon had a deal to buy the property that would become Hidden Valley Homes II.

The only problem was that we were already overextended with the other two developments. We decided to get out of the $900,000 foreclosure property, which had already been partially developed by someone else. Before too long we found another buyer and, boy, were we relieved.

The day we were supposed to close the deal, I woke up to a front-page headline in the local newspaper that changed everything. A child had been molested in the clubhouse that was already on the property, and everybody in town was talking about it. The man who was going to buy the land from us backed out of the deal.

Not really knowing what else to do, we called Bank of America and asked them if they'd take less for the property if we paid them in cash. They said they'd take 10% off the price, which saved us $90,000. That discount made it a lot easier for us to do all three deals at the same time.

Another way we offset some of the cash flow problems we created by taking on all three projects at once was to build 50 homes in Hidden Valley Homes II instead of 30. To do this, we had to get the city to change the zoning from R1-10 to R1-6, which meant reducing each lot in the development from 10,000 square feet to 6,000 square feet. It took us six months to get the change through the zoning board. If we were trying to do the same thing today we would have been dead in the water, because now a zoning change like that takes at least five years.

We were lucky that everything worked out as well as it did with these three projects. We were able to pull them all off because we knew what we were doing when it came to the actual building, and because we were able to think creatively to overcome the obstacles that were put in our way.

After we got comfortable building large subdivisions, Art and I saw an opportunity to capitalize on a new trend in home building. We noticed in the late 1980s that there was a growing demand for houses on larger pieces of land. We thought this would be a tremendous opportunity for us, especially since many of our previous customers were having families and were looking for larger homes with a little more room to breathe.

In 1988, we built a subdivision called Paradise Mountain Estates. It contained 50 homes on spectacular, two-acre lots. The property was incredible, and I snapped it up without even showing it to Art. It was 125 acres of dead avocado trees, high up on a hilltop. Most people only saw the dead avocado trees, but I saw the potential for a beautiful neighborhood.

At the time, we were one of the only builders in North County doing big-lot subdivisions. Naturally, we were a little bit nervous about trying something that hadn't been tested in our area, but we just knew in our guts that customers would find the concept attractive.

As part of our marketing plan, we decided to contact all of our previous customers and tell them about the new opportunity to own a Duncan/Crews house on two acres of land. The response was great because these people knew we were going to build them a quality product, and they were excited about having extra space for their kids, dogs, horses, and gardens. We offered a $3,000 incentive to our former customers (the houses cost about $190,000) and gave them first pick of all the lots. We sold 11 units right away, or about 20% of the total, which was a great way to start the project.

Paradise Mountain Estates was a huge success, and since then we've never turned away from the two-acre lot concept. There's still a big demand for this type of home in North County.

One part of our business did change in the early 1990s, and it was pretty dramatic. After 12 years of building homes together— about 800 houses in total—Art decided that he needed a change of scenery. I felt devastated. I felt like we were getting a divorce. I tried to convince him to stay, but he insisted on moving on.

There were two or three months when things were a little tense between us, but our friendship pulled us through and we were able to work out the logistics of the business. We remain best friends and still do business together today. We own commercial buildings, industrial buildings, shopping centers, and oil wells—among other things—and we're always looking for new opportunities to do deals together.

When Art moved to Texas in 1993 and stopped building, I took what was left over in California and Duncan/Crews Development became Michael Crews Development.

Today, it's typical for us to have about 12 projects going on simultaneously. But it still all comes down to building each individual house to the best of our ability. My customers don't care how many other houses we're building, they care about the house they're going to move into. That's why I put such a huge emphasis on quality craftsmanship and customer service in running my business. In fact, it's our mission to build homes of exceptional quality and value, and to be committed to customer satisfaction.

That mission applies to each and every home we build—not some homes, not every other home, not only the most expensive homes.

My big thing is that we've got to get each house perfect before a customer moves in. I've been beating this into the heads of my co-workers so much that they can all probably tell it to you in their sleep. If a house is 100% perfect on the day a family moves in, the only thing we'll hear from them is how much they love their house. If a customer moves in and their house is only 95% perfect, then they'll never leave us alone. Never.

I'm so concerned about perfection that I make it a point to personally go through each house we're building every week. We call it "Crews Control." I'll do this before hours, after hours, and whenever else I can find the time. I'll put Post-it Notes around the house, wherever I find problems or have questions. When my team comes back to work on the house, they'll see all my notes and can address any problems right away. Or I'll record my comments into a tape recorder and share them with the team later on. Either way, usually about 80% of the things I notice are already being handled, so it's really more of a double check than anything else.

The more houses we build, the harder it is for me to get to all of them, but I think it's an important thing to do for a number of reasons. First of all, I can put a fresh set of eyes on a project, and with years of experience under my belt I really know what to look for.

Second, knowing that I'm going to check on things helps motivate the people who work with me to do the best they can do. They're not afraid that I'll come down hard on them, they just know that the fewer problems I find, the more kudos, recognition, and rewards they'll receive.

Third, the people I work with feel better knowing that I care about all the details. They like that I'm hands-on, not some absentee business owner out on the golf course. They appreciate the fact that I care about the work they're doing, and they know that if I find any problems I'll work as hard as I can to help fix them. Often, the people on my team will thank me for noticing things and for preventing them from slipping through the cracks.

Doing the extra work we do to make our customers happy makes all of our jobs easier in the long run. This has long been my philosophy about work—doing the best you can minimizes problems and maximizes the return on your investment of time and energy.

Because of our commitment to quality and service—the natural results of hard work—Michael Crews Development does an exceptional number of repeat sales. People aren't usually brand loyal when it comes to houses, but we have customers who are on their third and fourth homes with us. We also sell a large number of houses to people in the real estate, mortgage, and construction businesses. These people see everything, and it makes my whole team proud that our houses are thought of so highly by people in the know.

I believe that the main reason we succeed as a hardworking team is because we really focus on what we're doing. Focus allows us to get better work done, because we're looking at every little detail. And it also allows us to be incredibly flexible.

If you look at any Michael Crews Development subdivision, you'll see a lot of variety. That's because we offer our customers a lot of choices. We can build pretty much any floor plan in any of our locations, and our customers can choose the style of roof and the color of stucco they want. If a customer likes one of our floor plans but prefers a six-car garage instead of a four-car garage, we can accommodate that too. I want my salespeople to have the flexibility they need to sell houses, because if they don't sell houses we don't generate any revenue, and nobody gets paid.

The flexibility we offer our customers ties into our company slogan—"No Boundaries." We want to be able to build anything anyone wants us to build, from a doghouse to the Taj Mahal. Whatever someone needs, we can do it, and we promise to do it well.

Having flexibility built into our business culture also makes it easier for us to adapt to changes and stay ahead of the competition. It's how we were able to pioneer the two-acre lot concept back in the late 1980s and dominate the market.

Not too long ago, two elderly brothers wanted to know if we could customize one of our homes to have two master suites and two separate entrances. They wanted to live together, but they both wanted their privacy. We did the work for them, and got to thinking that there may be an increased demand for this type of living space. So now, as part of our regular floor plans, we offer one called the Quincy. It's a two-family house with two master suites and two separate entrances—and it's selling. This year, we expect to build a handful of these houses, and I anticipate that demand for this type of home will increase dramatically in the years ahead.

By recognizing building trends early, we enjoy several advantages. We can build a few houses based on each new idea in the beginning, learn from what we're doing and work hard to perfect the system, and then be ready to fly when demand takes off and before the competition catches on.

In addition to my core development business, I've started a number of related businesses that support my home-building efforts. Michael Crews Development has a few new divisions today, including a painting division, an options and upgrades department, and a realty division through which we help customers buying one of our new houses sell their current house. I've also started a mortgage company, I'm involved in a bank, and I opened an escrow company. My philosophy is that if I use a product or service every day to help me run my business, then there's a good chance that it would be to my advantage to own that product or service.

Over and above the businesses that support development efforts in North County, I've also expanded operations to other cities with hard workers I've grown to trust. Paul Tyson Seivert is operating Tyson/Crews Development in Phoenix, Arizona, and in our first year of business we're doing between eight and ten beautiful homes. That's big for a first project in a new city. Don Olson (no relation to my former real estate boss) is spearheading South Fork Estates in Seattle, Washington, a 76-unit subdivision.

And then there are businesses I'm involved in just for fun. I already mentioned some of the deals Art Duncan and I have done together. In addition, because of my passion for flying, I started an air charter company with another airplane buff, Steve Brower.

Brower Crews Air Charter offers a terrific Cessna 421 CW twin-engine aircraft that's regularly hired out by bank executives, winery owners, farmers, and even other real estate developers. This service gives greater flexibility to businesspeople than scheduled commercial flights, and we're able to go to all kinds of locations that traditional carriers can't. Our chief pilot, Mike Lane, is a retired Navy pilot who's both hardworking and personable, and all of our clients really love and respect him.

Being a hard worker has allowed me to branch out in lots of different business directions, and it's incredibly rewarding for me to help other hard workers do the things that they're meant to be doing. In return, I hope that the people I help can help other hard workers someday, too.

So that's basically how I built my career—step by logical step, attainable goal by attainable goal. I've always worked hard, and I've always looked for opportunities to move up to a higher level without putting too much at risk. Sometimes circumstances forced me to take bigger jumps than I would have liked to have taken, but for the most part I've been pretty strict about not overextending myself.

If I had to sum it all up in one sentence, I'd say that consistent hard work and gradual improvements over time are the keys to business success. Slow and steady wins the race.

In the sections that follow, you'll learn more about why hard work is so important, and how you can harness the power of hard work to achieve great things for yourself, your family, your co-workers, your customers, and the greater community.

I was just an average kid from a small town who refused to be put down by society. The things I've done aren't so unusual, but the fact that I've done them is unusual. I find it sad that success and happiness seem so elusive these days, because we live in a world that holds out great opportunity to everyone, if we would only do the work that's required.

Most people try to do too much too soon, or they don't stay focused, or they get discouraged, or they don't work hard enough, or they don't get out of bad situations and look for new opportunities. I'm here to tell you that tremendous success is possible no matter who you are, and I guarantee that if you put in the effort and approach your career the right way, you'll be able to achieve an amazing level of success.

PART II

The Rewards of
Hard Work

"MUCHO BUENO," I SAID in broken Spanish. "Mucho bueno!"

Luis smiled and nodded his head. He was excited and filled with
pride in a job well done. "Mas trabajo?"

I had a lot more work for Luis Feria back in the early 1980s. He
was so good, I couldn't afford not to keep him busy. If I didn't
have work for him on a construction site, then I'd find something
for him to do at my house.

Back in those days, we picked up Mexican laborers early in
the morning in front of an orange grove on Mountain View Drive.
There were about 40 guys there who lived under orange trees or
inside a run-down old garage. Luis Feria was among them, and

he called one of the orange trees home. When it rained, he'd make a shelter by tying a big piece of plastic to his tree. And every morning, he'd smell like fire and smoke because he did all of his cooking outside in a makeshift firepit.

Luis and the other guys had all risked their lives to cross the border, so they could make money to send back to their families.

We paid those guys $30 a day. Luis would send $28 of it back home, but he was a lot more disciplined than most of the other guys.

From the very first time Luis hopped into the back of my pickup truck to work for me, I knew I had to find a way keep him around. Every day, he'd be waiting for us in a big group of guys who wanted to work, and I made sure that he was always one of the guys we took to the job site. My truck would be mobbed every time I went to that orange grove to pick people up, but we usually only needed four or five guys. Some of the guys who mobbed the truck were probably really hard workers just like Luis, but I had to turn them away because we only needed so many people. Other guys never got picked a second time because they were lazy or just couldn't understand what we wanted them to do.

Because of the language barrier, we had to demonstrate tasks and hope the guys would be able to get them done. We always gave them more to do than they could in a day, because we wanted to make sure they were busy. Even so, 95% of the time we had to watch the guys like a hawk or they'd hardly get anything done.

But not Luis. I'd give him something to do, and I'd come back later and it would be done perfectly. And then I'd ask him to do something else. Sure enough, I'd come back and it would be all ready. Luis is one of those rare people who can understand a job after only one explanation and figure out how to get it done. He was smart enough to solve problems for me, not create them.

"Mas trabajo?" was always his smiling question when I came around to check on him.

More work. "Mucho trabajo for you, mi amigo!" was always my grateful reply.

I told Art, my partner, "Man, I keep picking up this one guy and he's a real good worker. He's nice, he's hustling—this guy wants to get ahead! We've got to latch onto this guy because he's just too good to let get away."

I picked Luis up every day, and he never let me down. He quickly caught on to everything we had for him to do, and he always wanted to learn new skills.

One day, he started asking questions about going to school to learn English. And before we knew it, Luis started taking English classes at night at the local high school. Soon, it became easier and easier for us to communicate and teach him new things. He was especially interested in irrigation systems, and he quickly became an expert in that area.

I don't remember Luis ever asking us for a raise, but every so often we'd give him more money to show our appreciation for his hard work. He always thanked us, and he continued to take the little he needed to survive and send the bulk of the money back to his family.

Luis got paid more because he was worth more to my business. He was always on time, he was honest, he took initiative, he worked harder than anybody, and he always did everything right the first time. He was aware of everything around him and looked for opportunities to get ahead. From my perspective as a business owner, those are great qualities for any employee to have.

Even though we were worlds apart in many respects, I saw a lot of the same values in Luis that were helping me build my own career. I had tremendous respect for his work ethic, and I wanted to help him succeed.

I met Luis more than 20 years ago, and he's been one of the best people I've ever had the pleasure of working with. He's now in charge of finishing all the homes we build, and everyone at

Michael Crews Development, especially the 30- or 40-member team he manages, loves him dearly.

After Luis was with me for several years, he went back to Mexico to get his wife and their baby. They snuck back into the country and moved into Luis's brother's apartment. Before too long, Luis and his wife started having more kids, and eventually they were granted amnesty and became United States citizens.

As Luis's family grew, one day I said to him, "Luis, I want to build you a house. Save your money, my friend, I'm going to build you a great house." He saved his money, and I found a beautiful lot on a hill for him, with a spectacular view of the Pauma Valley. We designed and built a special five-bedroom house for his family.

The guy who was once living under an orange tree now lives high above the orange groves—that's what can happen when you work hard!

When I realized that Luis's 20th anniversary with my company was approaching, I decided to do something really big for him. At the Michael Crews Development Christmas party in 2002, I gave Luis a beautiful new Dodge Ram truck.

Each year, we put on a special presentation as part of our annual Christmas party, which is held in a large banquet room. When people came to the party that year, they were greeted by this big blue truck with a big red bow around it.

I remember pushing that truck into the party room with the help of Ralph Capuano, my customer service superintendent, while a woman from the banquet facility sat behind the wheel. We had to push the truck through a narrow hallway that only had about an inch to spare on either side of the truck. To protect the floor, we used two bed sheets. Ralph and I would push the truck five or ten feet, move the rear sheet to the front of the truck, and then push some more until the truck was finally in position.

I'd do anything for Luis, and this was going to be his night! I had pictures of Luis doing different jobs from over the years blown up into huge posters, and we put them on easels all around the truck to celebrate his long and wonderful history with our company.

When it was time to make the official presentation, I stood in front of 400 people—employees, contractors, and their significant others—and said, "You know, Luis, when you work someplace for 20 years, sometimes they give you a watch—if you're lucky. Well, my friend, I got you a clock for your 20th Anniversary— and it has a whole truck built around it!"

I showed more pictures of Luis's life, including the orange tree he lived under when we first met, and told everybody the story of how he rose up the ranks of my company through hard work.

"Luis," I continued, "you've been an inspiration to me and to all of us at Michael Crews Development over the years. I want you to have this truck."

Everyone in the room stood up and applauded this quiet, hardworking man who had accomplished so much in his life and brought so much joy to thousands of home owners in North County. I don't think there was a dry eye in the house after the presentation, and we went on to have one heck of a party. It filled my heart with joy to see Luis so astonished and happy that night, and I was honored to be able to show my appreciation for a truly special human being.

But the fun and amazement didn't end there. Near the end of that same evening, we planned to raffle off a Harley-Davidson motorcycle. We were doing it to raise money for a charity that my wife and I started for the purpose of helping hardworking families deal with unforeseen tragedies (you'll read more about this in chapters 7 and 24). We sold 20 raffle tickets for $1,000 each.

Before the party, Luis told Mike Daghlian, our top grader, that he had to buy a ticket. Luis, in his quiet, unassuming way, was a big proponent of this effort and I think he sold more tickets than anyone.

"Okay Luis," Mike said. "But if I buy a ticket, you have to buy one, too!" Luis agreed, and they decided to share the Harley if either of them won it.

Well, the planets must have been all lined up that night, because Luis won the bike. It was absolutely unbelievable. All the other guys who spent $1,000 on tickets said that if it wasn't going to be them, they wanted Luis to win the bike.

As a fitting ending to a remarkable evening, I remember putting the Harley in the back of Luis's new truck and watching him drive off.

What a night!

Luis's story is probably the most dramatic example of what can happen when you decide to work hard and focus on long-term success. His dedication to hard work and his ability to focus on any job he was given went a long way toward improving his lot in life. Luis Feria's work ethic helped his family, it helped his co-workers, it helped my business and our customers, and it gave me wonderful opportunities to help him even more in return.

When you commit yourself to working hard, the rewards are tremendous—and they never seem to stop coming your way. Hard work sets in motion a marvelous, continuous cycle that keeps spiraling upward, allowing workers and customers to keep having more and more great experiences.

Imagine if every worker in this country was like Luis. Imagine if *you* were more like Luis. I believe we'd be a much more productive and prosperous nation, and that people would be happier.

The sad thing is that people like Luis are the exception rather than the rule, when it's really very simple to work hard.

I'm continually fascinated by the results you can achieve through hard work and focus, no matter where you are in life. If you asked most people where they thought a homeless man— who lived under an orange tree and couldn't speak English— would be in 20 years, they probably wouldn't imagine him living in a five-bedroom house with his wife and kids, earning the respect of his co-workers and customers, making a good salary, and driving a brand-new, cherried-out pickup truck.

The remarkable power of hard work is that it actually makes your life—and your job—easier by allowing you to achieve great things. Luis's story is the perfect example of this. The harder he worked, the more he achieved, and the easier his life became. It was hard work that allowed him to move from the orange tree into a beautiful house on a hill with his loving family. It's true that it didn't happen overnight, but it did happen. Luis took charge of his own destiny and did the work he needed to do to succeed.

I can virtually guarantee that if you really work hard consistently for the next five, ten, or twenty years without worrying about the results or getting upset by the success of others, you'll look back on your experience fondly and you'll be amazed at how much you've achieved.

You can work your way up to an incredible level of success, but you have to do the work. I know that doesn't sound fun, glamorous, or exciting, but in the end it can be all of these things. Hard work may look like an oyster sometimes, but its rewards are like a beautiful, shiny pearl.

Some of the rewards of hard work are tangible, like money, power, fame, recognition, or your name on the new wing of the local library. Other rewards, however, are more difficult to define and almost have to be experienced to be truly appreciated.

I believe, for example, that you're better able to discover a purpose for your life when you work hard. This is an incredible reward, but it's difficult to understand when you don't already have a purpose in life. I'll try to describe it for you, but you've just got to trust me that it feels terrific.

I'm sure you've probably experienced a great sense of accomplishment on various occasions in your life, like in school when you aced an exam, on the tennis court when you beat a tough opponent, at home when you assembled a piece of furniture, or maybe even in your business life when you got a promotion or figured out a solution to a problem.

Well, when you work hard consistently, you kind of get that same amazing feeling all the time. Everything you do gives you an incredible sense of winning accomplishment because you're constantly looking at the bigger picture of your life, and are constantly savoring even the smallest victories. As a hard worker, you know that each of your experiences is contributing something to a purpose for your life that's larger than you are. It's a hard-work high that infuses you with incredible confidence and energy, and a tremendous zest for life.

It's too bad that we don't remember all the things we had to do when we were babies—like learn how to eat, crawl, walk, and talk. Now *that's* hard work! And yet, we did it purposefully. Sure we cried sometimes, but we got over it pretty quickly and got right back to work, not worrying about how much we were getting paid, what other babies were doing, or how much vacation time we were accruing. We enjoyed the process as much as the results. And if we had loving parents giving us encouragement with each little thing we did correctly, we were motivated to work even harder.

Once adults commit to becoming hard workers, they're often amazed at their capacity to be productive, and they're amazed at the happiness and fulfillment that their productivity creates in them. Once again, a wonderful spiral is set in motion—when you focus your energy and attention on your job or career, you get more done, gain skills and confidence, see how your work helps other people, make career advancements, experience joy, and get even more energy to focus on your job or career.

My biggest pet peeve these days is that young people in their teens and twenties just don't seem to know how to work. No one seems to be teaching them how to do it. They drift into the office, store, restaurant, or wherever they're "working" whenever they feel like it. They don't take pride in what they're doing, and they expect the world in terms of salaries and benefits. Work to them is just killing time until the weekend—and they wonder why they're not succeeding!

People who know me are well aware that I have no tolerance for laziness, and that I reward hard workers generously. Recently, I gave a job to a young man who had an intimate knowledge of how great a company Michael Crews Development is to work for. All he had to do was work hard and he would have secured himself a long and profitable future with my company. But the kid couldn't even get to work on time!

"I overslept," he'd say.

"Then don't go to sleep if you're going to forget to wake up," I'd reply.

I talked to this guy on three separate occasions, and three times he told me that he'd get to work when he was supposed to. He blew it each time, and I had to let him go. He gave up a great opportunity that could have changed his life, just so he could get a couple extra hours of sleep—which he could have gotten by going to bed earlier.

I honestly don't understand the mentality that allows people to shirk their responsibilities to an employer, or to themselves for that matter. In my opinion, not working hard is complete and total self-sabotage.

If you have to spend eight, nine, or even ten hours at a job each day, why not make something great out of it? Why not use that time to reward yourself and others through your hard work?

One summer when I was in high school, I worked for Art Duncan's father, Darryl Duncan. I was helping him plaster walls. I never thought twice about getting there before Mr. Duncan did and getting everything set up so we could get started as soon as he arrived. And every day after "quitting time," I'd clean up and move the scaffolding and other equipment over to the area we were going to tackle the next day. No one asked me to do this—it just seemed like the best way to get as much done as we possibly could.

These activities only took about a half an hour each day, but they helped our productivity skyrocket. It was a small thing to do for a huge result, and Mr. Duncan rewarded my efforts with praise, bonuses, and good references to his bankers years later, when Art and I decided to start our own home-building business. The payoff for this extra little half hour of hard work was enormous.

Over the years, I've learned that if you work hard for people without any expectation of reward, the rewards come your way in droves. They may come to you in strange or unexpected ways, but they do get there.

I remember getting a call one day from a sweet elderly lady, who asked me if I could build a 600-square-foot house for her and her husband on their daughter's property. She had gotten the runaround from several mobile home companies, and finally called me out of desperation.

The property was really hard to get to, and I knew we weren't going to make any money on the deal, but I told her that we'd do it. We maintained the same high level of quality that we always do, we worked hard, and we ended up building a terrific little house for this nice couple.

It was all part of our "No Boundaries" commitment to building whatever the customer wants. At the very least, it was a nice thing to do for some nice people. We gave the keys to the woman and she thanked us for the wonderful house, and to be honest I didn't give it much thought after that.

But then a strange thing happened. We started getting calls from people who were referred to us by this sweet lady. Lots of calls. Lots of great calls. And even to this day, she's a great source of excellent referrals.

I can assure you that hard work does pay off. If you're patient and diligent, the rewards will come. Sometimes what seems like a lucky break can only occur if you put in weeks, months, or even years of hard work.

Working hard is an investment of time and energy that can provide you with tremendous returns. Like any investment, it requires taking a risk and hanging in there for the long term, but in many ways it's a sure thing.

In the next few chapters, I'm going to describe some of the specific benefits of hard work, using more examples from my personal experiences. As I said in the beginning of this book, if I knew what the rewards of hard work were going to be when I was getting started, I would have worked even harder than I did.

5

Hard Work Can Make You Rich

I WAS VERY SERIOUS when I met with my father that day.

"What's up, son?" he asked.

"Mr. Olson said that he'd only hire me if I promised to commit 100% of my time to real estate," I began.

"That shouldn't be too hard for you," my father replied. "I taught you how to work hard!"

"He also wants me to have six months' worth of living expenses in the bank so I won't worry about money in the beginning."

"What do you think about that?" my dad asked.

"He just wants to know that I'm committed, but that sure is a lot of money. I know I can do great when I get focused on something." There was an awkward pause.

"How much do you need?" he asked.

"Four thousand dollars."

That was a small fortune for my dad. I knew he didn't have the money to throw away, and I suspect Mr. Olson came up with that six-month figure just to get me out of his hair.

"Can I borrow $4,000 from you, Dad?" I could only ask because I knew that I'd pay him back, no matter what.

"Of course," he said. He could only say yes because he knew that I'd pay him back, no matter what.

My dad gave me the money, and I walked into Mr. Olson's office with my bank statement in hand. I think he was surprised to see me, but he was a man of his word and he hired me on the spot.

My dad never said anything about the money–he never had to. Right away, I started paying him back–$1,000 a month for the first four months I was in the real estate business.

I never had to ask my dad for money again.

Money has always been important to me, but it meant a lot more to me when I was just starting out than it does now. Money is probably important to you, too, or you wouldn't be reading a book about how to get ahead.

Achieving success these days is synonymous with getting rich. Most people who want to succeed in business dream of having enough money to do whatever they want, whenever they want to do it. They want luxury cars and fancy houses. They want to take exotic vacations, stay at magnificent hotels, and dine at five-star restaurants. They want to be millionaires or even billionaires.

All of this is possible through hard work. Money is a great motivator, and it's one of the most obvious rewards of working hard.

I get irritated when people say negative things about money, things like, "Money is the root of all evil." That's nonsense. The actual quote from the Bible is "The love of money is the root of all evil," which I take to mean that greed can interfere with living a decent, happy life. Money itself is neutral, and you can do a lot of good things with money, such as pay and reward hard workers, produce products and services that customers want and appreciate, and give to worthy causes.

Another negative thing that people say about money is that "money can't buy happiness." This may be true, but in my opinion too deep a belief in this idea tends to limit people's opportunities to earn money. If you don't think money can make you happy, you let yourself off the hook and don't have to work hard to try and make money. I think a better view is to see money as something that can help you do more of the things that make you happy, including helping others. If you're already happy (or if you know what makes you happy) and you have money, it's a pretty good combination.

Money allows people to do fun, exciting, and noble things, and it has a lot to do with being comfortable. And I don't just mean personal comforts like a nice home, a safe car, and good food. It also has a lot to do with your comfort on the job. When people work hard and are paid fairly for their efforts, they tend not to worry about money so much—which allows them to do their jobs better, work harder, and make even more money.

When you worry about money, you can't do your job effectively. That was Grant Olson's lesson to me when I started selling real estate. He wanted me to have six months' worth of living expenses in the bank and quit all my side jobs so I wouldn't get distracted by money while I built my career as a realtor. He knew that if I could focus my full attention on my hard work, the money would take care of itself. He was right.

Many people are impatient when it comes to money, and they get frustrated with work when they don't build up their bank accounts fast enough. Other people convince themselves that no amount of hard work could possibly get them to where they really want to be financially, so they resign themselves to mediocrity. Either way, the money they wish they had remains a fantasy.

It can be difficult in today's world to have a realistic view about money, because there's so much unbelievably big wealth around us. It seems as though we read or hear about how much money Bill Gates, Tiger Woods, Oprah, and other business, sports, and entertainment celebrities are making every single day. Our perception of wealth is influenced by the media's obsession with the richest among us. The wealthiest people always seem to be the ones most written about and most talked about, leaving everyone else feeling like failures.

It all depends on how you look at things. We all can look at Bill Gates and not think we're rich. But did you know that if you make $117,000 a year, you're actually among the wealthiest 10% of all households in the country? Did you know that you're considered rich by the IRS if your household income is $92,000 a year? And did you know that if you make $42,500 a year, you're among the wealthiest 50% of all households in the country?

When you're starting to work hard and are starting to get ahead, you should definitely think about how much money you want to make and what you want that money to do for you. The sky's the limit, but you should also think about things that might come before you make your first million or billion dollars—things like getting out of debt, buying a house, or paying for your kids' education. Think about how much money you make today. Would $50,000 a year be a big improvement? A hundred thousand dollars a year? A million dollars?

When I was starting out as a hard worker, all I wanted was a lot of money. The reality of my situation as a water-tank delivery guy making $2.80 an hour should have made me give up my ridiculous goals, but I knew that if I was patient and persistent, I could accumulate great wealth. I had a surefire plan— hard work.

The problem with most people who want money is that they don't know what to do or how to go about getting it. Part III of this book will give you a plan of action you can use to become a hard worker and make all kinds of money, whether you work for yourself or someone else.

I always knew that if I worked hard, I'd be okay financially. As long as I had an able body and an active mind, I knew I could provide for my family, save for the future, and build wealth. I kept proving it to myself over and over again each time I received a paycheck or scored a commission. In the beginning the amounts might not have been that big, but that really wasn't the point.

The harder I worked and the more opportunities I took advantage of, the more money I made. Making money motivated me to find even more opportunities. All the side jobs I had, like my paper route and selling vegetables, were all important components of my quest for cash when I was younger. I took Mr. Olson's advice and gave up all those jobs because it was important for me at the time to really focus on one new career; but I look at my life today and again I'm involved in all kinds of different side jobs. I'm even growing grapes on my property to sell to different wineries. There's not a lot of money in this, but I really love the work involved in setting up this new business and can get pleasantly lost in it.

I never really wanted money so I could spend it on extravagant things. I've never been a real flashy kind of guy, although I admit that I did buy a brand-new BMW when I was managing the real estate office in Poway.

For the most part, I was taking such pleasure in my work and in getting ahead that the idea of spending money on vacations, clothes, or dinners out all the time just didn't appeal to me.

I even looked at vacations as opportunities to make money when I was in my 20s and 30s. I once owned a cabin up in Big Bear Mountain, a popular weekend retreat about two hours north of San Diego. Instead of going to hotels or spending money on a motor home that went down in value, I bought a cabin that went up in value. I rented out the cabin when my family wasn't using it, and sold it after a few years for a nice profit. The cabin cost me $25,000 in 1980, and I sold it in 1983 for $75,000.

The real reason I wanted money was because I saw it as the way businesspeople keep score. For me, earning money has always been like scoring a touchdown, hitting a home run, or making a three-point shot at the buzzer. Making money represents winning, and beating the other guy in a fair and healthy competition has always been an important motivator for me.

I don't care where you are in your career or what you do for a living, your work becomes a lot more fun and exciting when you see the money you earn as points in a big game. I got the same thrill when I made $15 commissions selling water-conditioning services as I do today when I sell $750,000 houses.

When you start equating the money you earn with your score in the game of business, however, be sure to focus on competing against your peer group, instead of wishing you could play in the same league as Bill Gates or Oprah right away. If you beat a friend at tennis you don't complain that you didn't win Wimbledon, do you? If you win a golf match you don't beat yourself up about not being on the PGA Tour, do you? It's the same in business. Savor every victory you achieve, because the small ones are just as sweet as the big ones if you have the right mindset.

Gradually, you'll be able to compete at higher levels. In fact, just looking at every dollar you make as a point in the game of business can have a powerfully positive impact on your ability to make money. Try it and see what happens. I'd be willing to bet that you'll start enjoying every penny you earn instead of complaining that you don't have enough. I bet you'll be motivated to earn more money by working harder and learning new skills. And I bet you'll be more aware of opportunities you can take advantage of to advance your career.

Keeping score with the money you earn allows you to have a dynamic career that keeps you fully and completely engaged in the work you do. It allows you to become a hard worker with focus and vision. And it allows you to negotiate better when it comes to money. I don't give raises based on tenure in my company. I learned this from Lee Iacocca. I give raises to people who are willing to take on more responsibility. When someone asks me for a raise, I ask them what extra value they're going to contribute to the company. And when I offer someone a raise, I let them know what extra work I expect them to take on.

As fun as it is to be competitive and look at your job as a game you can win, you've also got to remember to be a good loser. It's a waste of time to be jealous of others who might be doing better. Use them as inspiration, like I used Tommy Hopkins and his Quota Buster Award record to make myself a better real estate salesman. Keep your focus on your job, and keep the competition healthy.

Hard work over time can bring you great wealth by increasing your income potential, but income is, for most people, only part of the complete financial picture. When you use your hard-work skills to invest some of the money you make, you not only prepare yourself for a future when you'll no longer be working, but you make your money work harder for you now to give yourself a better future.

This isn't a book about investing, but I do want to talk about it briefly because investing has a huge potential to make you wealthier than you can be from job income alone.

Personally, I believe in real estate so strongly that I put money into houses the way people put money into stocks and bonds. Even if you have to buddy-up with your friends, I believe that real estate is the way to go when it comes to investing money. I'm in the land business, and I can tell you that they're not making any more land.

Land naturally becomes more valuable as populations increase, and it becomes even more valuable as environmental and other groups apply pressure to preserve it. New rules and regulations are making it more expensive to build new buildings. For example, in order to have a septic system approved on one particular project, we had to agree to hand-dig the system and preserve the native grasslands on either side of it. This meant hand-carrying nearly 1,000 feet of pipe and heavy tanks, which costs a lot more time and money than bulldozing the land and trucking in the materials. Fortunately, my son Justin had a creative inspiration and suggested that we hire a helicopter to fly in the materials. We saved some money and a lot of time, but it still cost more than usual and we still had to charge more for the homes we were building.

Because the cost of new housing is going up, the cost of existing houses is going up, too. In my opinion, the prices of new houses always drive up the prices of older houses. Older houses will still be cheaper, but they'll rarely be much of a bargain in a tight market. Most people want to buy new if they can, but developers can't build new houses fast enough to meet the demand. So the short supply of new construction drives prices up higher overall.

My point is that I think real estate is a good investment, and I definitely put my money where my mouth is. I even put other people's money there, too.

About five years ago, I came up with a unique benefit that gives the members of my A-Team profits from different real estate deals. The A-Team consists of about 17 great contractors who've been working with me for a long, long time. They're all extremely accountable for their work, they never cover up problems, and they work really hard to help me build my business. I really wanted to help these guys build up some money for retirement, but since they weren't employees I couldn't set up a formal retirement plan for them.

So I decided to help them by investing in real estate. It started out with the construction of a single house. The members of the A-Team worked on the project and got paid for it just like they would on any other Michael Crews Development project, but the difference was that they also owned the house. When the house was sold, all the profits were put into an account just for the A-Team. This past year, we bought some land in the town of Vista that can hold five homes. Michael Crews Development is absorbing some of the costs of the project, and all the profits on that deal will go to the A-Team, too.

Some of the A-Team members were skeptical about leaving their money with me like this, but so far they've each been able to accrue about $25,000. If a guy's smart, he leaves his money in the account, lets it grow for the future, and lets me invest in bigger and better real estate deals for him. I've got to tell you, these guys are pretty smart!

So that's my quick case for real estate, but it's in no way meant to be specific investment advice. Just like stocks, not all real estate deals are a sure thing. You'll want to research different types of investments and figure out which ones are best for you. Just take a hard worker's approach to investing for your future— focus on what you're doing and don't take risks that'll get you in trouble if things don't happen the way you hope they will. You may even want to look at investing as a big game, just like your job, so you can get actively involved in winning.

Hard work can bring you lots of money, as long as you realize that you're the one in control of your own destiny. There are lots of people who look like they're working hard and aren't getting ahead financially, but don't let that fool you. When you work hard and continually look for new opportunities, you're sure to achieve a level of financial gain that will make you more comfortable and allow you to do more of the things in life that make you happy.

6

Hard Work Enriches
Other People

I WAS HAVING ONE OF THOSE DAYS
where I was getting slammed at every turn. It seemed like everything
that could possibly go wrong went wrong at the same time. Unexpected and heavy rains were causing expensive construction delays, an
important deal fell through, a client was complaining to us about something that wasn't our fault, one of my best people was out sick, and I
banged my knee on my desk.

I work hard enough when everything goes right–and now I have
all this other stuff to deal with?! "Why don't I just give it all up?" I thought
to myself.

Then I noticed the letter on my desk. It was from a customer who
had recently purchased three houses from us.

"Dear Mike," it began.

"Now that the dust has settled somewhat, I wanted to take a
minute to let you know how much I enjoyed working with MCD in the

building of my family's new homes. I, like anyone contemplating building a new home, had heard all the horror stories–cost overruns, subs not complying with the plans, endless delays, stress, and strain on personal relationships...

"I am pleased to report that I had none of these experiences. We built two houses and a guest house on time and on budget. This is not to say that there were not problems or mistakes along the way. However, any mistakes or problems that did arise were resolved quickly and handled professionally.

"Marc and I love our Heston IV. It is just the right size for us, our three-year-old, and our many pets. We love the open flow of the house and the large windows that let the outside in. Also, the dining room is big enough to accommodate our dining room table which seats 18 for dinner parties. The Princeton is great for my parents. The house has plenty of room for them, their health care assistants, large dogs, and the occasional guest without feeling too big....We also really enjoy the guest house. Its current use as a home office is great, but it has the flexibility to be a caretaker's quarters should my parents ever need 24-hour care.

"I also wanted to take a minute to thank the members of MCD that took extra special care of me. I am so glad you put Sam on my project. Sam is an honest and conscientious person and it was a pleasure to work with him. If Sam did not know the answer to one of my questions, he said so and then immediately found the answer. I am really going to miss my weekly meetings with him. You of course know how great Mary is. I always knew that she watched your money like it was her own, but I really got the feeling that she watched mine the same way. It was so nice having Denise in-house to help with all our finish choices. She had great insight and really helped me to cut where I could cut and blow the budget where it would make the most impact. I hate to not mention everyone, the framers, the painters, Pablo, Bob, and Ralph who were all great to me.

"I also had the pleasure of working with several of your subs that cannot go without mention. Jim Kelly of Skelly Electric, well what can I say? You know how fabulous he is....Jim's lighting suggestions were right on. Randy Hoff at Dreamscape convinced me to put speakers throughout the three homes, and what a nice touch that has been for the several parties we have had since moving in. Bob and Lance Gremett did a fabulous job on our cabinets and matching built-ins. Bob really took his time going through the houses with me and making suggestions for some of the special things I wanted. Denis Hobson did such a nice job at a great price on our driveways, we hired him to pour our pool decks and build our outdoor barbecue. While we had some challenges getting the plumbing fixtures all just right, the guys at Valley Center Plumbing kept coming back without complaint until everything was done. The window and door guys, the roofers, and the mason all did nice jobs.

"Your suppliers were also obviously well chosen and very helpful. Mike Stangle at Standards of Excellence had lots of suggestions for my appliances and plumbing fixtures, and I am really glad I took his advice. Christy Effendi at Arizona Tile spent hours and days with me picking the tile for the three houses. Gary Richards and Bruce of Gary's Tile also sat in on these long meetings, which was extremely helpful. Again, I hate to not mention everyone since I did not have a bad experience with any of them.

"Let me just offer my congratulations; you have a great team. I would and have recommended MCD to my friends and family. Thanks again, for everything."

That letter made my day, and all of my problems suddenly seemed insignificant.

I get great letters from customers all the time, and they always make me feel like my hard work means something important.

There's nothing like a satisfied customer to give me the energy to keep working harder, or to save the day during those rare times when everything seems to be going badly.

While I compare money to the points an athlete scores on the playing field, I consider satisfied customers to be the equivalent of wildly enthusiastic fans. (I know this chapter is about making *other* people feel good, but I have to tell you that it's personally rewarding to have satisfied customers.)

When I work hard and my customers are happy, then my hard work has directly enriched their lives, in addition to bringing me money and pride in a job well done.

The more satisfied customers any business has, the more demand there is for that business's products or services, and the more money that business can make. Financial gain is usually highly dependent upon customer satisfaction.

When I started building houses with my friend Art Duncan, we worked hard to build the best houses we could in the first-time homebuyer's price range. That hard work paid off when potential customers shopped around and realized that a Duncan/Crews house was going to enrich their lives more than another builder's house.

Hard work allows you to build a superior product or offer a superior service that pleases more and more customers. This is what our free market economy is all about, and it's how a "little guy" can often beat the "big guys" and even become a "big guy" himself one day.

So first and foremost, hard work enriches the lives of customers. This may seem ridiculously obvious, but it can be easy to forget if you don't have direct dealings with the customers of the company you work for. When you can't see the human faces that your job ultimately has an impact on, it's much easier to complain about your job, minimize its importance, and give your job less than your best effort.

No matter how distant a job is from actual customer contact, it still contributes to the overall satisfaction of a business's customers. That's why I believe it's so important for every person in every company to have an amazing work ethic.

In addition to customers, there are other people whose lives can be directly enriched by your hard work, and you see them in person every single day. These people are your co-workers, and can include your boss or manager if you have one, your employees if you have any, and anyone else who works with you. The people who rely on your performance are enriched because your hard work helps make their jobs easier, and your energetic involvement helps build camaraderie. Even people who aren't directly affected by your job can be inspired by your example and by the rewards you receive because of your hard work.

I know that many people work at companies where hard work is hard to come by. But that shouldn't stop you from being a hard worker. It'll probably be difficult to be the only one working hard. At first, people may be threatened by your new attitude, and they'll certainly try to drag you down to their level of non-work. But I can guarantee that if you persist, your hard work will go a long way toward improving the overall experience at your place of business.

When hard work takes over the workplace, everyone working there becomes happier and the benefits ultimately extend back to the customer. This is exactly what happened when I took over the real estate office in Poway, and it's why hard work really is the easy way to achieve success.

While every working person can enrich the lives of co-workers and customers directly through hard work, I believe that setting an example of hard work and helping employees become the best they can be is the responsibility of any good manager, boss, or business leader.

When I can take a person with little or no training at all and help build that person up to one of the highest levels of management in my company as I did with Luis Feria, that's big stuff. It's big for me, it's big for the person I'm helping, it's big for his or her family, it's big for the other people who work with me, and it's big for my customers.

I try to help everyone who works with me reach their full potential so they can fully enrich their own lives and the lives of others. It's a process that my wife Kelly has dubbed "upbuilding:" guiding people (including yourself) through continuous career advancement. In Part III of this book, you'll learn more about how the upbuilding process works to help hard workers achieve greater and greater levels of success.

My hard work, and the hard work of each of the people who work with me, has helped thousands of people fulfill the American Dream of owning a home and has generated livelihoods for many hard workers. I recently figured out that it takes about 400 different people to complete one of my houses, from breaking ground to the day we give the keys to the customer. Back in the 1980s it was just Art and I, but our hard work allowed our business to grow and enrich the lives of more and more people.

It's pretty amazing when you think about what might have happened if I had stayed at the water company for a few years, hurt my back, and collected disability. I would never have touched so many lives so positively through my hard work. I know that's an extreme example, but we all make the same type of decision every day when we go to work. Do we sit around and do nothing, or do we work hard and potentially affect the lives of hundreds or thousands of others in a positive way through our efforts? Even if we just make one person smile because of how hard we work, it's worth it.

My son Justin once had a basketball coach who only had one leg as a result of a motorcycle accident. Before the accident, he was a great ballplayer. After losing his leg, he could have easily given up on life, but instead he decided to use his knowledge of the game to work hard and enrich the lives of others.

By becoming a coach, he figured out a way to stay involved in the sport he loved. He really got caught up in the games and was amazing to watch. He'd move up and down the sidelines, barking instructions and encouragement to his players and watching the referees like a hawk. He was so good, you didn't even notice the crutches, or the fact that he only had one leg. What you did notice was how much energy he had, how attentive he was, and how his team rallied behind him and gave him 150%.

I know this incredible person was unhappy about his accident, but he rose above feeling sorry for himself and built a career that not only enriched his own life, but also the lives of his co-workers (his team) and his customers (all the team's fans).

Whether you're an employee, manager, or business owner, you have countless opportunities to enrich the lives of others directly through your hard work. And when that hard work becomes second nature to you, it naturally spreads beyond the realm of your co-workers and customers into the community at large.

7

Hard Work Improves
The Community

A SMALL GIRL LOOKS UP in the sky, smiling from ear to ear as the colors explode in the darkness. Brilliant reds, bright whites, and dazzling blues, plus magnificent greens and pinks and oranges fill the night sky.

It's the Fourth of July in Valley Center, California.

"Wow!" says the little girl.

Her dad reaches down and pats her on the head.

There are nearly 6,000 people gathered in the football field of Valley Center High School, celebrating their country, spending time with their families, and enjoying the fireworks show.

Before my wife Kelly and I got married, we tried to watch fireworks from my backyard one Fourth of July. As we looked up into the sky in anticipation of a great show, our fun and romantic idea quickly fizzled out. All the fireworks were too far away!

Kelly looked at me and said she wished that Valley Center had its own fireworks. I agreed. People in Valley Center had to go to Escondido, Poway, Oceanside, or San Diego if they wanted to catch a display.

"Why don't we do something, Michael?" Kelly suggested. "I bet we could put on a terrific Fourth of July celebration for our town."

The more we talked about it, the more excited we both got. I was behind the idea 100%, and Kelly took the ball and ran with it all the way into the end zone. She talked to fireworks companies, worked with the local fire department, and talked to the school district about letting us use the high school football field. It was a huge undertaking, but in 1999 Valley Center had its very own Fourth of July celebration, fireworks and all.

Half the town showed up when the doors opened at five o'clock in the evening. Kelly organized gunnysack races and other contests for the kids—everyone who participated got some kind of ribbon or trophy. A band played and people actually danced in a special area that was roped off for dancing. Face painters got squeals of delight from the kids. Our enterprising sons, Tyler and Justin, made money selling glow necklaces. Football games sprang up spontaneously.

Admission was free, and we invited people to pack up their picnic baskets and spread out on the grass. Some of the local community groups set up booths and sold food. The only things that weren't allowed were alcohol and tobacco, since we were using school property.

To be honest with you, we wouldn't have had it any other way. There was another festival in town that relied heavily on beer for people to have a good time, and we wanted to be different. We wanted to be totally opposite. Our mission was to do something wholesome for the town—and people really appreciated it.

They appreciated it so much, in fact, that they expected us to do it again the following year—and the next, and the next, and the next. We kind of thought it would be a one-time thing, but people were having such a good time that we decided to make it an annual town celebration sponsored by Michael Crews Development.

The event has grown each and every year, and we now put on the second largest fireworks display in North County. The high school cheerleaders run the games and races for the kids, organized by age groups—3 to 5, 6 to 9, and 9 to 12. The football team mans the biggest rock-climbing wall in the county. Clowns make balloon animals. We even have a dunk tank for local notables like the coach of the football team and the vice principal of the high school. Everyone tries to get me in there, but I keep telling them that I've got to work!

Thousands of people enjoy the evening on the football field, and thousands more enjoy the fireworks from their own backyards and porches. One man came up to me and told me that he lived next to Disneyland for 15 years and had never seen such an incredible display of fireworks. Another family told me that they drove in all the way from Oceanside because they heard how great the Valley Center fireworks were.

Valley Center, California, is a great place to watch fireworks on the Fourth of July. At nine o'clock, the band starts playing *America The Beautiful*, the fireworks start exploding in the clear summer sky, and all is right with the world.

It's such a charge to know that all of this came about because of hard work. The hard work of the people in my company, who generate the money to sponsor the event, and the hard work of my wife and her team of volunteers, who make the event come alive.

When you work hard in your career, you tend to work hard in other areas of your life. And when that energy spills out of the office and into the community, thousands upon thousands of people can benefit.

In addition to the Fourth of July event, Kelly runs a charity called HOME, an acronym for Helping Others More Efficiently. It's yet another way that my wife and I use the fruits of our hard work for the greater good.

For years, Michael Crews Development would get invitations to help this or that charity, and it got to the point where we were simply handing out checks. We wanted to do something a little more meaningful, so in 1998 we decided to sponsor a charity concert to benefit the Boys & Girls Clubs. Kelly got in touch with a few talent agents and ended up hiring country singer Toby Keith who put on a spectacular performance. We raised a lot of money for the kids, but after we handed over the check, that was that.

While we were happy to help such a worthy cause, we felt that it would be more personally satisfying to be more directly involved in where the money went. Kelly did some research, and discovered that there was an opportunity to help people in North County who had the same kind of hardworking mindset as we had.

If you're a typical working person in this country and something bad happens to you, like cancer or a heart attack, you're not eligible for any kind of aid from the government. You'd be surprised to find out how hard it is for families in America to get help when tragedy strikes, even when they have insurance. We thought that America's hardworking men and women were worthy of assistance, so we set up our charity to help such people who are struggling with hardship caused by illness.

HOME provides funds to help families get back on their feet. And, because we know the recipients of the money are hard

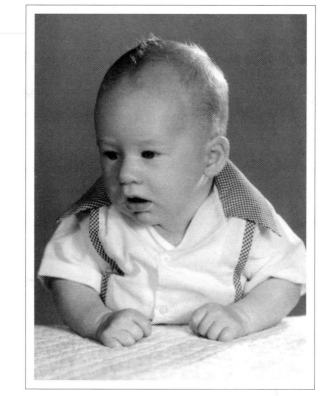

A hard worker in the making, 1956.

With mom, dad, and sister Nikki, around 1963.

With my dog Gemini, tilling the soil so I could plant corn and sell it, around 1968.

Taking a break from picking oranges, around 1972.

Walker Scott Little League Team portrait, 1966.

Picked for the Escondido Little League
All-Star Team, 1968

Little League gave me a competitive spirit
and taught me a lot about effective teams.

Eighth-grade sports award ceremony at Orange Glen
Elementary School. Rick Weaver and I won first place in
two-man basketball.

A fight to the finish, 1973. Bob Peavey was the only guy faster than me on the Orange Glen High track team.

As wide receiver for the Orange Glen Patriots, 1973. Baseball Hall of Famer Duke Snider thought I had a bright future in football.

Orange Glen High varsity basketball picture, 1974.

On the court for Orange Glen
High against El Capitan.

Senior portrait at
Orange Glen High,
1974. I was ready
to start working!

This 1978 football program I sponsored as a real estate agent contained a picture of my future wife
Kelly, on top of the human pyramid. We wouldn't meet for 19 more years.

Making it big in real estate, 1978.

Moving the house I bought for $500, 1980.

Pulling the house onto its new home.

Watch your step! Coming out of the house after securing
it on its new foundation.

The first trailer Art Duncan and I bought held all our equipment and a small office, 1981.

A Duncan/Crews promotional flyer, around 1985. One of the rare photos of Art and me together.

Sign for Hidden Valley Homes, one of Duncan/Crews Development's first big subdivisions.

Aerial shot of the land we bought from Cheech and Chong, taken from my B-55 Barron.

Mike Zajda's son with an ostrich egg in the Valley-Tex Farms incubation room, 1993. Mike, Art, and I were going to be ostrich farmers, but a virus wiped out our herd.

Luis Feria, 1999.

The orange tree Luis Feria called home when we met in 1981.

Luis with a Ditch Witch at Silver Oaks, around 1994.

Sign for a subdivision
named after my
eldest daughter.

My house, just after completion in 1996.

Custom home built for one of
my old high school basketball
teammates, 1999.

A Michael Crews Development house in
Bonnie Lake, Washington, 1997.

The Development Team, 1999.
(Back row, left to right: Luis Feria,
Manuel Leon, Russell Ahonen,
and Sam Hernandez. Front row,
left to right: Pablo Rivera,
Rod Wisma, Mark Duncan,
Moose Cleary, and Sergio Anaya)

Michael Crews Development
group photo, 1999.

The Development Team, mid 1990s.

Pablo Rivera working hard, mid 1990s.

My assistant, Mary Bradley.

Denise Sherr, Karen Roslie, Mark Connal, and Faith Ashford.

Minutes after proposing to Kelly in Hawaii, 1997.

Wedded bliss, 1998.

Having fun with my daughter Sky, 2000.

With Kelly's son Tyler (left), my daughter Ashley, and my son Justin.

Justin at age 18, in front of the first house he built and sold for a profit, 2001.

Tyler bodyboarding in Chile, 2002.

With my 1997 Road King Harley, 2001. I raffled off the bike to raise money for HOME.

Kelly, pregnant with Jet, 2003.

My dad, Ken Crews, relaxing in Zion National Park.

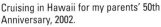

Cruising in Hawaii for my parents' 50th Anniversary, 2002.

Ken and Erlene Crews, around 2001.

Taking a well-deserved break with Ashley and Justin, 2003.

Sky on Freckles, 2003.

Flying high with Justin, 2001.

Kelly and I with title company representative Greg Whistler and his wife Mary, skiing at Mammoth Mountain, 2003.

With Ashley, welcoming guests to a
luau at my house.

A-Team member Dave Popoff
and his wife Janet.

A-Team member Mike O'Donnell with
his wife Carole in Tahiti, 2002. Mike played
basketball with me throughout high school.

Kelly and I with A-Team members
and their spouses.

A-Team spouses enjoying some Tahitian
hospitality. (left to right: Cathy Gremett,
Janet Popoff, and Maggie Fuller)

workers, we ask that they repay the money back to the charity someday if they can. This is by no means a requirement, and we don't put any pressure on people to repay the money. We do this only to inspire the people we help to help others in return, if and when they're able to do so.

What's amazing about this charity is that the people we help never have their hands out. After one special woman named Norma Eckblad was diagnosed with cancer and faced huge medical bills, for example, she was embarrassed to ask for help even though she needed it. She and her husband run their own landscaping business. Her treatment was an enormous expense, and the illness forced both her and her husband to work less. Norma felt badly about not being able to work, and about not being able to bring in the money they needed to pay the extra medical bills that weren't covered by their insurance.

Friends told Norma about HOME, and at first she was skeptical. But after she talked to Kelly and realized what the organization was all about, she filled out the application and thanked us profusely for the help we were able to give her.

Norma Eckblad is one of the success stories. Her cancer is in remission, and she's fighting back with a great chance of returning to her normal life. She's back at work, and continues to help our cause by referring more and more people to HOME.

While Norma's story gives us reason to celebrate the work we do on behalf of hardworking families, other stories don't have such happy endings. Norma referred us to a man she met while she was getting treatment for her cancer, for example. He was a self-employed electrician who couldn't get any aid. He told Kelly that he had to make a choice between getting his medicine and leaving something behind for his family. This brave, loving, and hardworking person ultimately lost his battle with cancer, despite all the love and support he got from his family and his community.

When things turn out this way, it gives me all the more reason to work harder and harder to help others. The sad stories make you appreciate the value of every human life even more than the success stories do, and they can have a positive impact by inspiring people to work hard for the greater good.

I want people to see my company and me donating back to the community in positive ways. Not because it's some marketing ploy to get more business, but because I want to bring the community closer together and show people how hard work can benefit our society. I want more people to express love and compassion for each other. I want more people to realize that we're all here on this earth together and that the time we share is precious.

I've been blessed in my life, and I believe that it's my obligation to give back to the people and the places that have helped me achieve my success. It's my way of saying thanks.

I enjoy helping the community I'm a part of, which in my case is Valley Center, California, and the entire North County area where I grew up. You might be more inclined to help a cause that transcends geographic boundaries. You may want to help find the cure for a particular disease. You may be interested in helping people of your particular ethnicity, race, or gender. You may want to help families, teach kids about exercise and nutrition, or help disadvantaged kids get to college or learn job skills. There are many worthy causes out there, and through hard work you can become a champion for the ones that tug at your heart the most.

8

Hard Work Feels Great

COACH MERRILL WENT TO THE PODIUM
at the annual Orange Glen Patriots Sports Awards Banquet in 1974. He was the coach of the varsity basketball team that year.

"I have a special announcement," he said.

Everyone quieted down, and all you could hear was the occasional clink of silverware on china.

"I have a special announcement about a special young man who'll be graduating this year."

Everyone looked around at all of us seniors. No one knew what was going on.

"As you know, each year we work hard to represent Orange Glen High School on the playing field," coach Merrill continued. "And we work especially hard when we're playing our cross-town rivals–the Cougars from Escondido High."

A chorus of boos rose from the audience.

"Well, there's one fine ballplayer in this audience who takes those games particularly seriously. His name is Mike Crews."

The crowd burst into applause, and I couldn't believe what was happening.

"If Mike scores 15 points in a normal game, he scores 25 points against the Cougars! If Mike usually gets two or three blocked shots, he gets six to eight against the Cougars! And if Mike typically gets 12 rebounds, he gets 20 against the Cougars! Mike Crews is what we call a Cougar killer!"

The crowd went nuts as coach Merrill unveiled a huge plaque with my name on it.

I was the first recipient of the Orange Glen Patriots Cougar Killer Award, and man, that felt totally awesome.

Every time I met the Escondido Cougars on the playing field, I played stinking out of my brain. It was such a big deal back then, because there were only two high schools in the whole town. Everyone showed up for these games, and when the two teams met it was the only thing anyone could seem to talk about for days.

Any matchup between the Patriots and the Cougars created a buzz throughout the town. People would be expressing all kinds of opinions and making all kinds of predictions. You could feel the anticipation in the air before each game. Larry Littlefield, the sports reporter for the *Escondido Times-Advocate*, would write incredible stories about the cross-town rivalry, before and after each contest. The first editions of the paper would come out at midnight every night, and after one particularly successful basketball game against the Cougars, I made my girlfriend stay up and come with me to see if my picture was in the paper. Luckily for me, it was!

The games themselves were spectacles. When the two teams met on the basketball court, it would be standing room only in the gym. The whole town wanted to come see us play, and I thrived on having everyone watching, cheering, yelling, and screaming. I played so hard because it felt so good to get the admiration of fans and the respect of players and coaches on both sides.

It's the same in business. When you work hard, you earn more respect and admiration, and that makes you perform better and please your co-workers and customers even more.

It feels great to earn money and make customers happy. It feels great when your customers tell you how much they like something you produced. It feels great when you and your co-workers are thriving. It feels great when you have the extra resources to help people in need. It feels great to win. It feels great to see people 30 years later who remember your performance in a basketball game against Escondido High. I don't think any of these things are secrets, but it's amazing how many people don't seem to get it.

I remember how one football coach tried to psyche us up for a game one time. We were all in the locker room, and he told us that we were going to be playing a tougher team, a bigger team, a team with a better record. "But you know something?" he said. "They're putting on their uniforms one leg at a time, just like you."

I understood what he was trying to tell us, but in the back of my mind I was thinking that I don't want to be a normal guy with two legs. I want to be everything that normal is not. I want to stick out. I want to give 150% when everyone else is only giving 75%.

I'm the first to admit that there are lots of things that I can't do very well, but I figured out early on that if I could work hard and get really, really good at a couple of things, I could have a personally fulfilling life.

In school, I picked sports over academics. As an adult, I chose real estate as my career. And I decided to fly an airplane as a hobby because it's a big challenge that requires a lot of hard work and focus. Flying is very stressful, but when you're focused on it, the stress actually goes away—just like at work. Flying is a great passion of mine. In fact, I'm so passionate about flying that I've even taken a lot of extra schooling to get a commercial, multi-engine instrument rating.

What makes hard work feel so good is the difference between just going through the motions and being passionate about something. It's the difference between playing any old basketball team and playing your heart out against the Escondido Cougars.

I encourage you to find something to be passionate about. It doesn't necessarily have to have anything to do with your work, but ultimately I hope you'll find a way to channel the kind of energy and enthusiasm that comes with passion into your career.

For now, just find something that you're so interested in pursuing or learning about that it completely consumes you for awhile. Start learning a sport, a language, or a musical instrument—your progress will make you feel great. Buy and fix up a condo or a house with some friends and rent it out—that first rent check will make you feel great. Be the best parent you can be—the love that you get back from your kids will make you feel great.

There are so many things you can do in the world for the pure pleasure of doing them. When you really get involved in something, you won't even realize how hard you're working. You'll learn to focus on the activity so much that you won't even think or worry about the results—the results will just be a big bonus.

By getting to that point with a hobby, pastime, or interest, you'll be able to see how working hard at your job can bring you to that same wonderful place in your career, where you'll feel great because you're engaged in what you're doing and enriching your own life, as well as the lives of others.

Try and get excited about your work—whatever your job is. Tackle each assignment head-on with intensity, enthusiasm, and determination, and give all the people you work with every reason to call you a Cougar killer!

PART III

Easy Ways To Work Hard

MY 19-YEAR-OLD SON JUSTIN announced that he'd be moving out of our house. It's not like I didn't know it was going to happen. He had already bought the house he was going to move into, but the closer he got to moving day, the sadder I became.

"I'm moving out on Saturday, and you're going to have to help me," he insisted.

"Son, I can't help you," I replied.

"Why not?" he asked, getting annoyed.

"Because I'll be crying all day long!"

I couldn't bear to see Justin go off on his own. It just seemed so abrupt, even after 19 years. If you're a parent, you'll understand–you want your kids to leave the nest, but it's definitely bittersweet when it happens.

I have to laugh at myself now, because Justin was only moving three miles away. But at the time I was in a bad mood.

"Suck it up, dad," he said, exasperated with his old man. "I'm leaving."

I pouted.

And then, in all seriousness and with great love, Justin said to me, "Dad, you know this is your fault–you made me what I am today."

Just like my father taught me the value of hard work, I passed the same lessons on to my son, Justin. I'm incredibly proud of the hardworking path he's chosen for his life's journey. It makes me happy to see how much he appreciates the value of hard work, and that he knows that his destiny is in his own hands.

Justin works in the sales office of my company one day a week, and he's out in the field five days a week, learning the role of superintendent. I want him to learn everything about my business, and he wants to learn it all, too.

In addition to working hard for me, he's also doing extra things on his own. He's already built two houses and sold both of them at a profit—far more than the salary he earns from Michael Crews Development.

Justin was 15 years old when I realized that my messages about working hard and looking for opportunities were really sinking in. You see, all our kids have the same deal from Kelly and me. We pay for half of their first car, and they have to come up with the other half. They can get any kind of car they want, and when they save up enough money for half of it, Kelly and I match the rest. But with Justin, it was a different story.

"I'm going to save up for a Rolls Royce or a Mercedes," he told me, a year before he was even going to learn how to drive. "And as soon as I buy the car, I'm going to turn right around and sell it."

"Why would you want to do that?" I asked.

"Because I really want the money so I can build a house."

I nearly burst with pride and joy, and I couldn't stop smiling for weeks.

"Son," I said, trying to contain myself. "Now listen. You don't have to go through all that. You save up your money and I'll match it so you can build your house."

Justin had been working hard for me since he was eight years old. He started out picking up trash and pulling weeds at job sites for $3.50 an hour and worked his way up to making $8.00 an hour framing houses. Plus, he was shrewd enough to borrow my car when he needed to get around town. By the time he was 17, he had enough money saved to start building a house.

Justin and I discussed different possibilities, and he decided which piece of property to buy and what kind of house he wanted to put up. He chose a one-story home with four bedrooms, three bathrooms, and a four-car garage. Justin chalked out the house on the graded pad, and decided to put in upgrades like granite kitchen countertops and additional landscaping.

I charged Justin a fee to help him build his first house—just like I'd charge anybody else. Six months later, the house was complete and he sold it for a pretty nice profit.

He used part of the money he made to start construction on another house, and we worked out a similar arrangement. As he was building his second house—without even telling me about it—he found another piece of land. This property already had a house on it (the one he moved into that made me so sad), and it also had room for another house. Talk about a chip off the old block!

Justin asked his uncle Scott if he wanted to live next door to him, in a new house they'd build together on the divided lot. They figured out the finances and became equal partners in the deal, and they're going to live on the property for three years before they sell both houses and move on to bigger and better things.

Watching Justin over the years has taught me that anyone can benefit from working hard if they make the decision to do it. I didn't have many material things when I was growing up, and that motivated me to work hard to achieve success. Justin has a lot more than I ever did, and my success could have allowed him to live well without working hard. But he has that same competitive drive that I have, and he's just as motivated as I am to make his own mark in the world.

Recently, Justin and my daughter Ashley both told me how much they appreciated the way I raised them. Justin in particular told me that the work ethic I instilled in him has made a huge difference in his life compared to other kids his age. This meant a lot to me, because until he was 15 all he did was complain about the work he had to do! Besides starting to work for me on job sites at eight years old, Justin had to do a lot of chores around the house. By the time he was 13, he was working for me on the job twice a week for six hours a day, and he was doing a lot of hard work at home. He often got mad at me, but now that he sees that so many of his peers don't have a clue about how to work, he realizes that working hard as a kid was a sacrifice worth making.

Anyone can achieve his or her own success through hard work. You just have to make up your mind to work hard—it's as simple as that. And there's really no excuse for not making that decision, unless, of course, you're already so content with your life that you don't need more money, don't need to have a purpose, or don't want to help other people.

"But what if I fail?" That's the biggest objection to hard work there is. I say, "So what?!" If you learn from your failures and don't give up, success is sure to follow. It might not always be the kind of success that you first imagined, but that's part of the wonderful mystery of life. Every hard worker I know can look back on his or her experiences—the successes as well as the fail-ures—and find something satisfying about them.

If you can maintain a positive attitude and continue to work hard even in the face of failure (or what initially appears to be failure), then I'm convinced that you'll have a rich and reward-ing life. It may be difficult to get started, but I can assure you that the more you work hard, the easier it—and your life—becomes.

In the following chapters, I'm going to share with you some of the secrets of hard work that I've learned over the years. If you can apply these lessons to your own career and truly adopt the atti-tude of the hard worker, ultimately you can't fail—even if you make a few mistakes along the way. I know that everyone's situa-tion is different, but I honestly believe that there's a distinct method to hard work that any working person can use to get ahead. It's a method that shows you how to minimize risk and maximize the return on your investment of time and energy at your job.

Simply spinning your wheels on busywork and not getting anything productive done doesn't qualify as hard work in my book. That's nothing more than a waste of time. I'm sure you've seen it in the workplace—people who *seem* like they're working hard but never actually do anything. That's not what this book is about. Why would anyone work hard if they weren't going to get something positive out of it?

I want you to reap tremendous rewards in return for work-ing hard. That's why I'm presenting all the actions you can take if you want to get ahead and do great things in your job, your career, and your life. Some of the actions I describe may seem obvious to you, but sometimes the simplest things are the first things people forget to put into practice. Others will hopefully be actions that you've never even considered and will really help to advance your career when you apply them.

I've put the actions you need to take to succeed in as logical an order as a printed book will allow, but you'll discover that there's quite a bit of overlap. I cover some of the same ground in more than one chapter, but hopefully this will serve to reinforce the most important points and make it even easier for you to understand what you need to do to create your own personal success story.

I've worked hard to write this part of the book, and I want it to do several things for you. I want this part of the book to inspire you to work hard at what you're doing right now, and I want it to show you how you can continually look for opportunities to improve your situation. I want this part of the book to help you minimize the impact of your mistakes on the job and maximize your confidence in your ability to take on more responsibilities.

I want this part of the book to make you aware of how the energy created by recognition, praise, and the achievement of manageable goals can propel your career and the careers of those around you to higher and higher levels. And I want it to show you how hard work can be one of the true pleasures of your life when you realize how completely your success and happiness is tied to the success and happiness of others.

When you work hard, you can achieve all the things we talked about in Part II of this book—money, a great feeling of purpose, and the joy that comes from helping your customers, your co-workers, and the larger community.

I can honestly guarantee that if you take any of the actions explained in this section, you'll be more excited about your work and realize that hard work is success made easy.

9

Find Something To Do

"THESE KIDS ARE LOST," I thought to myself.

I looked at the classroom of about 50 college students. They all signed up for this business class to get ahead, but they didn't look like they were going anywhere.

The kids were fidgeting and goofing around, slouched down in their chairs, or just plain asleep. There was little if any energy or focus in the room.

I began to talk and could see that my message wasn't getting through. I knew what they were thinking. "Who is this guy?" "What does he know?" "Do I really have to sit through this?"

Then I drew a rectangle on the white board in front of the classroom. I drew a line down the center of the rectangle. And I told the story of how I bought a house, divided the lot, bought another house for $500, moved it on the property, and made a profit of $40,000.

That story gets them every time.

The students sat up. They stopped talking and started to pay attention. They began to see that if they worked hard, they could achieve great things. They wanted to make a profit of $40,000, too!

I pointed to a kid in the first row and said, "You're the captain. You and the five kids sitting behind you are all going to buy a condo and start renting it out."

"We can't do that!" they said.

"Don't tell me you can't do it," I replied. "If you six kids don't get together and do it, then get a group of your friends together and do what it takes. You don't have any more time to lose. If you buy a condo and start renting it out, you can start earning money that's going to help you in the future. And if you don't want to buy real estate then do something else. But for God's sake, do something!"

I told these kids that *they* are the only ones who have any power over their own destinies. I told them that while they may think that the power is going to come from their employer, they're the ones who are going to have to get up every morning, perform, and compete to keep their jobs and advance their careers. It's always up to them, even though it doesn't seem like it all the time.

By the end of the class, there was a great energy in the room. The kids came up to me and asked all kinds of questions about what they could do to get ahead.

I could barely get out of the room, and when I finally did the kids followed me out to my car in the parking lot.

Every time I talk to a group of college kids, it's the same thing. They start the lecture lifeless and bored and end up with a lot of desire and enthusiasm. This tells me that, while most kids are totally lost when it comes to what they're going to do with their lives, all they really need is a little encouragement to understand that they can do great things.

I imagine that a lot of adults are floundering when it comes to their careers as well. It saddens me to think that people are just drifting along, bored with or angry at their jobs, when they could be focused on success and on something that they really want to be doing with their lives.

Having a vision for your future and being focused on what you're doing is big-time important. But it's an awesome responsibility, and it can scare a lot of people. The good news is that it's a lot easier when you break it all down into incremental steps and keep doing things along the way.

I break my achievements down into short-term accomplishments and long-term successes. My vision remains true to my long-term plans, and I focus my attention on the more basic tasks that I need to perform every day to get closer to achieving my goals and dreams.

In my early days, my vision was vague—I just wanted to make money. But then, as I got older and gained experience, I kept refining my vision. I wanted to be a great salesman. I wanted to sell houses. I wanted to manage other realtors. I wanted to have my own business. In each case, I had to focus my attention on all the little things that I needed to do in order to reach those bigger goals.

When I talk about finding something to do, I mean it on several levels—everything from finding something to do right this very second to finding a larger purpose for your life and career over time.

Finding something to do can begin the next time you go to your job, and it usually involves finding ways to work harder. It could be as simple as asking your boss for more responsibility. Or cleaning your desk. Or organizing your files. Or coming up with a way to do your job more efficiently.

I've always found that the more I do on a job, the faster it seems to go and the more satisfaction I get out of it. Many people who don't like their jobs would like them a whole lot more if they were just simply doing more when they got to work. People who have a lot of time on their hands in the workplace tend to be the ones who complain about their jobs, feel trapped, or drift off into a stupor. As the saying goes, "Idle hands are the devil's playground."

No good can possibly come from a job at which the person working does nothing. There was a guy working on a pretty sizeable job at my house one time. He knew that he'd get a big paycheck when he was finished, but every time I saw him he wouldn't be doing anything—all he ever did was complain to me about his financial problems. It got so bad that I finally had to let him go because he wasn't getting anything done. If he put the same amount of energy into doing his job that he did in complaining about money, he would have been able to take care of his financial problems!

His mother must have thought the same way I did. Apparently, she gave him a good talking to, and a few days later he showed up with a much better attitude. We gave him another chance, he did the job, my life was enriched by his work, and he earned his money.

So the first step toward success would be to try to fill your time at your current job with work. Not busywork, because that's just as bad as doing too little, but productive activity that yields results, enriches the lives of your co-workers and customers, and really engages you in your work. This type of focus on meaningful activity will guide you toward doing what you need to be doing, and will give you greater energy and confidence. If it leads to recognition, a promotion, or a raise—so much the better!

Finding more to do at work sounds easy enough, but it can be challenging. As I said before, some of your co-workers might feel threatened. Your boss might be too busy to train you to do a new task. You might get discouraged if your efforts aren't recognized. You might make mistakes. You might get tired or find ways to procrastinate. If you work at a place that doesn't have a hard-work culture, there'll probably be a thousand different obstacles in your way if you're trying to take on more responsibility. This is the hard part, but if you can persist enough to push through it, you and your entire business will work a lot more effectively.

Finding more work to do at the job you're doing right now is important, even if you're not going to be doing that particular job forever. Starting to work hard today helps you get into the habit of it, so you can really turn it on when you discover your life's calling. Think of your current job as a free laboratory for experimenting with the actions—and learning the lessons—of hard work. Think of your current job as paid training for your future success. If you're currently out of work, take any kind of a job you can find and learn from it. Take advantage of any opportunity you have to work hard right now, and you'll be amazed at how much better prepared you'll be to take on new challenges and achieve great things as your career advances and finds its true direction.

I knew that I wasn't going to deliver water tanks my whole life—my poor back just couldn't take it—but the opportunity that job gave me to practice being a salesman taught me many valuable lessons. It taught me how to contact as many people as I possibly could, how to keep track of all my prospects, and how to work with people once I connected with them. If I hadn't worked as hard as I did at Rayne Water Conditioning, I wouldn't have been able to give 150% to the real estate job that really launched my career and allowed me to become a success.

Hard work builds on itself and becomes a lifestyle that can lead you to great achievement. So start where you're at right now. When your days on the job are filled with productive activity, you're in a much better position to decide whether or not you really like your job and whether or not the job you're doing is the right job for you.

When you find more things to do at your current job, you don't have to stop there. I think there are great lessons to be learned from finding extra work to do outside of your main job. Living in Southern California, it was natural for me to sell fruit and vegetables on the side. And my paper route worked well for me because I had the early morning hours available to do extra work. I didn't need much sleep because I was so excited about making money and about making a name for myself.

When you're looking for extra work, you're going to have to figure out what works for your particular schedule. There might be additional opportunities at your current place of employment, as there were for me at Rayne Water Conditioning. Or you could do something totally unrelated to your job. What are you good at? What are you interested in? What's available in your area?

Maybe you need to do something mindless like stuffing envelopes to wind down from a day of intense mental effort at the office. Maybe you can get a paper route like I did or work at a retail store during the holidays. I don't care *how* old you are. Maybe you can make party cakes and sell them to your co-workers. Maybe you can import clothing, design jewelry, or build furniture. Maybe you can give guitar lessons, take wedding pictures, or write magazine articles. Maybe you can get involved with a multi-level marketing company. Or maybe you can do what my son Justin is doing and buy real estate and sell it for more than you make at your job.

We're not necessarily talking about starting your own business here, although side work can certainly lead to that. You never know what's going to happen with the things you decide to do on the side, but try not to think that far ahead. Just have fun trying things out and work hard while you're doing them.

The real reasons for taking on extra work are to help you learn how to be a more efficient hard worker, to allow you to earn extra income (and therefore score more points in the game of business), and to show you how it feels to be so busy that you don't have time to spend money recklessly.

First, let's talk about efficiency. I know that working harder at your current job and finding the time and energy to do even more work outside your job to make extra money is going to be challenging, especially if you haven't been working hard all your life. It's okay to take it slow in the beginning. This should be a learning experience, and you don't want to burn yourself out before you start seeing how hard work can pay off for you.

Think about how you currently spend your time. Are there any unproductive activities you can replace with extra work? Do you watch too much television every night when you get home? Do you sleep in too late on the weekends? Could you be more efficient at your job so you don't have to stay so late? I think you'll be surprised at how much room you can open up for hard work, even if it seems impossible right now.

Finding the time for extra work will help make you a more efficient manager of your own time, and it'll help you set your priorities. You may remember the story I told you about how my parents made sure that working never interfered with my schoolwork and sports. Trying to balance everything made me a lot more efficient, and I got to the point where I was hiring other kids to help me pack strawberries so I could go to baseball practice.

When you fill up your calendar with extra work, time really becomes a valuable asset. You force yourself to become more efficient while you're working, and you end up filling the rest of your time with things that are really important to you.

The second reason to take on additional work is to make more money. Even if the checks you get are small, it's amazing how great it feels to get extra money on a regular basis.

You can do a lot of things with the money you earn from extra jobs. You can use it to get out of debt. You can stash it away until you save up enough money for a down payment on a house or a condo. You can save the money for retirement. Whatever you do, make it a positive investment in yourself and your success.

This leads us to the third reason to take on extra jobs, to make yourself so busy that you don't have time to spend your money frivolously. When you're working really hard, often all you have time to spend money on are your bills and food. You'll be amazed at how just spending money on the things you really need can dramatically improve your financial position.

When I was working at the water company making less than $6,000 a year, my family was just getting by. When I started selling real estate my salary increased ten times, but I still didn't really spend any more than I was spending before. Because I was so busy, the money just kept on accumulating.

My growing bank account spurred me on to keep working hard, and it took me nearly 15 years before I started spending any kind of serious money on things like vacations. The funny thing is that all those years I never even felt deprived. I was having too much fun on the job and was thoroughly enjoying the rewards of my hard work.

Finding more work to do outside your job is a daunting task for some people, but I think it's an important thing to do. Just make sure that your side jobs don't interfere with your current employment. If you're just starting a career that you absolutely love, however, I may suggest you don't take on any side jobs. When I started out in the real estate business, Mr. Olson told me to quit all my other jobs so I could focus my complete attention on selling houses. That was good advice, because I knew I had found my career path (although, as I mentioned earlier, I'm back to my old tricks again and have more side projects going on now than I've ever had before).

You simply have to look at your situation and make a decision. For me, having those extra side jobs for so long in my late teens and early 20s helped give me the energy to devote 150% to the real estate business. Working extra jobs on the side is a great way to strengthen your hard-work muscles when you're just starting out, and it's a great way to share the rewards of hard work with others when your success has already been established.

I want to give you a few more words of caution about extra work. It sounds obvious—don't spend more money than you think you can realistically make—but you'd be surprised how many people ignore this advice. When people get excited about something, they often buy a lot of supplies and equipment, and then they lose interest. That's putting the cart before the horse. A friend of mine once spent thousands of dollars on video equipment, thinking he'd start a video production company. He was excited in the beginning, and the equipment was easy and fun to get, but he was unwilling to master the details involved in starting this new enterprise. The side business didn't pan out and he was out thousands of dollars.

When it comes to side jobs, unless you're already an expert at something or the initial start-up costs are minimal, let an employer worry about the overhead.

Whatever you do at your main job, and at any other side jobs you take on, always keep your eye on your ultimate goals of financial success and purpose through your work. This will help you get through the difficult steps in the beginning of juggling your time, finding energy, and setting your priorities and will ultimately enable you to discover the unbelievable joy that's waiting for you on the other side.

When you start replacing unproductive activities with productive ones at your current job, and when you start taking on additional work at different side jobs, you'll start seeing results quickly. Money will be coming in, and you won't have time to waste it. You'll spend more of your time doing more meaningful things. And sooner or later, you'll be happier about your work. You'll be so energized that you'll feel like nothing can stop you. I know this sounds impossible, but when you experience it you'll see the truth in it—trust me!

One weekend when I was about 25 years old, I went to a class in Los Angeles to learn how to buy real estate for no money down. The three-day class cost a couple hundred bucks. When the instructor introduced himself, he joked that by Sunday night, we'd all have purchased houses with no money down.

Only I didn't know he was joking. I was so focused on learning how to buy a house with no money down that I took him seriously.

Sunday night rolled around and the instructor was reviewing all the things he taught us over the previous two days. When it was time for our dinner break, he threw a newspaper down on his desk and said, "If anyone wants to buy a house now, here's the newspaper." Then he just kind of laughed.

Everyone else went out to dinner, and I made phone calls. I started calling people who had "For Sale By Owner" listings in the newspaper, and eventually reached a guy who was motivated to sell his house as quickly as possible. I told him that I'd buy his house right now if he'd give me the 6% he would have had to give a real estate broker as a commission. That way I'd have a down payment, and he wouldn't have to worry about selling his house anymore. He was interested, and I drove down to his house in Long Beach to figure out the details. I didn't even know where Long Beach was!

The class started up again as I was negotiating the deal on this house. The four people I came to the class with were getting worried because I hadn't returned to the classroom, and no one else knew where I was.

Finally, I walked back into the room with a big smile on my face. The instructor asked me what I had been doing, and I told him all about the house I bought in Long Beach.

"What?!" he said.

I can still remember the perplexed look on his face.

I didn't know what the big deal was. "I bought a house—just like you told me to do!"

When you're focused on a task, you charge. It doesn't even matter what the task is. When you find something to do, lots of times you do it.

10

Use Your Gifts

THE HOUSEWIFE OPENED her front door and saw me standing there with a big vacuum cleaner and a sleeve of golf balls.

"Good afternoon," I said with a smile.

She looked at me a little suspiciously. I was 17 years old.

"Do you have a few moments to learn about the Kirby vacuum cleaner?" I asked. "If you let me demonstrate this incredible machine, I'll give you these golf balls as a free gift to thank you for your time, even if you don't buy the vacuum."

If she let me in, I knew I'd be able to make a sale. The Kirby vacuum cleaner was an amazing piece of machinery. In addition to getting dirt off the floor, it could shampoo carpets, sharpen drill

bits, wax the car, polish the silverware, and do just about everything else except wash the dishes.

As amazing as the Kirby vacuum cleaner was, however, I was
an even more amazing salesman. Sales always came easy to me,
even at an early age when I was selling produce and showing my
parents' home to prospective buyers, but it was my experience
with Kirby that proved to me that I was really, really good.

I signed up to be a salesman for Kirby during the summer
after my junior year in high school. I went to a training class, and
everyone else was at least twice, if not three times, my age. A
sales trainer showed us how to demonstrate the vacuum, we were
told how to approach prospects and deal with objections, and we
were given a supply of free golf balls to hand out to people whose
homes we visited. We even sang songs to get pumped up and
motivated to be great salespeople for Kirby.

I ate this training class up because I wanted to learn all I could
about selling Kirby vacuum cleaners. I was extremely good at lis-
tening, and I hung on to every word the trainer said. I figured
that the trainer wanted me to succeed, so he must be telling me
stuff that worked. If the Kirby organization was willing to tell me
the best way to sell their vacuum cleaners, then it was to my
advantage to listen, focus, and learn how to do the job.

The vacuum cost $700 retail, and I got to keep about $90 for
every unit I sold. I was going to make a killing. After a couple of
months, however, I stopped selling Kirby vacuum cleaners.
School was about to start again, but the real reason I quit was that
selling Kirby vacuums made my stomach hurt. I was great at selling them, but all I was really doing was convincing people to buy
something they didn't need.

I was too skilled a salesman for my own good, and that often
backfired on me. I don't know how many calls I got from irate
husbands who couldn't believe that their wives spent $700 on a
vacuum cleaner. They'd yell at me and demand their money back.

Not only did I lose my commissions, I also had to go back to their houses and pick up the vacuum cleaners!

So while my experience with Kirby didn't go exactly how I expected it to, it was incredibly valuable because I realized that I had a gift that I could use to get ahead. The experience made me believe that I could have a career in selling, as long as I found something to sell that people really needed and wanted—like a beautiful house to live in.

My short stint with Kirby taught me to play to my strengths. Many people do this naturally, but I know lots of people who get involved in businesses just to make a buck, even though they're not suited for the activity. In my opinion, that's a real big waste of time, like staying in college would have been for me.

But we're told to do things that may or may not be right for us all the time. We're told to go to school, to work for a corporation, or to get involved in "get-rich-quick schemes." Have you seen some of the infomercials they have on television? You can order kits and packages that will help you make millions selling real estate, placing classified ads, etc. If you watch these infomercials closely, you'll notice that the emphasis is always on how fast you can make money, not on how great the products or services are!

While it's certainly possible to make money this way, I have to tell you that the number of people who buy these kits is a lot higher than the number of millionaires created by the kits. That's because most of the people who buy into these schemes are mesmerized by the promise of a big return without thinking about the work they need to do. The kits arrive in the mail, and the recipients soon realize that they're either not good at the activity or that they just can't put their hearts into it, which, as we talked about in Chapter 8, is an important motivator.

If you want to make a lot of money and you see an ad for a sales position, you're not going to make a lot of money unless you're a good salesperson to begin with, or unless you're so passionate about becoming a good salesperson that learning effective sales techniques is easy and fun for you.

Not everyone is a great salesperson, and not everyone wants to be a great salesperson. There are great builders, like my buddy Art Duncan. There are great administrators, like my assistant, Mary Bradley. There are great athletes, writers, doctors, teachers, lawyers, and accountants. There are lots of ways to succeed in the world.

The trick is to figure out what you're good at, discover what you're interested in learning about, and continually work hard to grow and improve yourself. You may have to try a few things before you hit on it, but you probably have a good idea as to where your natural abilities lie.

If you don't, there are ways to find out. Some people recommend thinking back on the things you liked to do as a kid for inspiration. Or you can ask your family, friends, and even your boss what they think your talents are. Or you can buy a money-making kit from an infomercial and see if it's the right thing for you.

In my opinion, one of the best ways to discover your calling is to find the activity that allows you to think less about the results of working (money) and more about the joy that can be had simply from the process of working. There's probably something that you do so well that you'd almost do it without even getting paid for it. Something that comes to you so naturally that it's inspiring for people to watch you do it or listen to you talk about it.

Have you ever watched Michael Jordan play basketball? It's a beautiful thing. Similarly, I can go out to a job site and watch someone frame houses for hours if they really know what they're doing. Watching someone who's using their gifts is an awesome experience, and it gives me a great deal of admiration for the many different talents that people can bring to the table.

I gained new respect for my friend Clark Bartram recently, after I went through the ordeal of shooting the photo that's on the cover of this book. Clark's a famous fitness model, and he's in front of the camera all the time. I used to think he had the easiest job in the world, but now I know how tough it is! He just makes it look easy because he's good at it. Playing cover model for a day was very difficult. Give me a hammer and nails, or give me a house to sell, and then you can see me use my gifts. While the photo shoot for the cover of *Hard Work* was uncomfortable for me, watching the photographer, his assistant, and the makeup artist do their jobs made the experience enjoyable. I was impressed by how hard and yet effortlessly they worked to get a cover shot we could actually use.

You may have heard the expression, "Do what you love, the money will follow." That's a little too New Age for me, but I believe in the idea in principle. If you do something that you're good at, or if you're involved in an activity that excites you and gets your attention, you're more likely to work hard at it, get better and better at it, find fulfillment because of it, and succeed.

11

Master The Details

"THERE'S A CHROME FAUCET in this house that hasn't been paid for yet."

That was the first thing Ralph Capuano, my customer service superintendent, told me after he completed his pre-walkthrough of this one particular house.

All I could do was smile. I was testing Ralph, and he passed with flying colors.

Ralph has had an interesting history with Michael Crews Development. He was a retired guy who bought a house from us, and after his experience as one of my customers, he asked me for a job. I was hesitant to hire him, but he was persistent. He told me that if I tried him out for a couple of weeks, I'd never want to let him go.

I remembered the real estate executives who said I was "too young" to sell houses, so I put aside my preconceived notions about how old a customer service person should be and gave Ralph a shot.

He started out part-time, but he soon became indispensable to me and my company.

One of Ralph's jobs is to walk through each of our houses and make sure that everything's perfect before we walk the customer through. He also has to make sure that any upgrades requested by the customer have been included in the house and have been paid for by the customer. It's a real detail-oriented position.

I knew that this one house had a chrome faucet in it that I had authorized personally, without filling out the usual paperwork. To make sure Ralph was doing a good job, I decided not to tell him about the faucet and see if he'd notice it.

"There's a chrome faucet in this house that hasn't been paid for yet," Ralph said.

That was all I needed to hear to know that Ralph could have a job at Michael Crews Development as long as he wanted one. He's so good at what he does that he even won our Leadership Award in 2002. When I presented the award in front of the entire company, everyone laughed real hard at the story of the chrome faucet.

When you find something to do and it's something you're either good at or passionate about, or at least something you can commit to doing to the best of your ability, then you're ready for the next step toward maximizing the effectiveness of hard work—mastering the details. This means knowing everything about what you're doing and, if possible, having first-hand experience with every task associated with your job.

As a home builder, I've done just about everything there is to be done to get a house built from the ground up. I've graded dirt for roads, poured concrete, and framed houses. I've dug trenches for irrigation lines. I've gotten permits from the city. I've installed appliances, woodwork, windows, plumbing, and electrical systems. I've even designed a few houses myself. I took the time to learn how to read blueprints and construction drawings, and I can look at a floor plan for a house and tell if it makes sense as an actual living space.

There are important reasons why you should master the details of your work—and the work of those around you. First of all, mastering the details of your job makes your job easier and frees you up to work harder. The more you understand about what you're doing, the more you can focus on productivity and efficiency—two great qualities for any businessperson.

When I went to the Kirby vacuum cleaner sales training class, for example, I knew that if I paid attention to what they were telling me I could start selling vacuums as soon as I walked out the door. If I didn't listen and understand their way of selling, I'd find myself on the job worrying about what to do, what to say, and how to act, and my sales calls would be a lot less productive.

When basic knowledge of a skill becomes second nature, it's a lot easier to perform that skill at a good clip when things are going well, and it's also easier to make quick adjustments if you're faced with unexpected problems.

In addition to allowing you to do your job better, mastering the details of your job allows your whole team to do better. Michael Crews Development takes a unique approach to building houses, which puts all of our superintendents on every house we build. Each superintendent handles a specific area. There's a superintendent in charge of getting the ground prepared, one in charge of framing, another in charge of finishing, and so forth.

Having specialized roles allows each superintendent to be more productive and efficient, because they have fewer details to master than someone who has to do an entire house from start to finish.

Finally, as you continue to master the details of your jobs as you advance along in your career, you become better prepared to be a good leader. If I hadn't mastered the details of every aspect of home building, I never would have come up with our system of putting several superintendents on each project. I wouldn't be able to look for mistakes or potential problems each week in every house we build. I wouldn't be able to sympathize with or be accessible to my co-workers. The people I work with aren't afraid to talk with me, because we speak the same language—the language in the details of our business that gives us a common understanding.

Mastering the details is a great way to minimize risk in any business. I couldn't have started my career by building a 100-unit subdivision—I would have been overwhelmed! But by learning all the details involved in building a single house, then two houses, then three houses, etc., I could take my knowledge and continually apply it on a larger and larger scale. By taking the time to master the details, you can make the impossible possible.

Mastering the details can be tedious and boring. But let me tell you, you'll get a lot more done in the long run.

You do things slowly in the beginning so you can really think things through and analyze what's going on. Through this process, you develop expertise. This expertise gives you the ability to constantly refine and improve what you're doing, and it gives you the confidence to learn new skills, build your knowledge, and advance in your career.

If you don't understand what you're doing or if you're not sure what's expected of you on a job, you're a lot less likely to enjoy your work and perform well. When I was first working with Luis and other laborers who had just come to California from Mexico, there was a definite language barrier. I didn't speak Spanish and they didn't speak English! So the workers had to understand visual demonstrations in order to catch on to what I wanted them to do. Anyone who needed verbal explanations to get a job done was at a big disadvantage.

In order to master the details, you have to be able to learn. I need to hear someone speak to me or see something demonstrated for an idea or a task to really sink in. If someone gives me a manual or a report to read, nine times out of ten my eyes will glaze over and I won't even see the words. It's important that you get exactly what you need from your boss or manager to succeed in your job. If you don't understand the details of your work, you may need to have things explained to you in a different way.

No matter what you do for a living, mastering the details is good advice to follow. It's a valuable activity that involves you and gives you renewed appreciation for your work. Try it for the next week. Go into the office, factory, store, restaurant, or wherever you work and focus on what you're doing. What are other people doing? How does what you do affect the work of other people? Are there ways you can streamline some of the things you do?

You may be surprised how much more interested you'll be in your job, how much faster the days will go by, and how much more you'll get done. You may be surprised to see how valuable even the simplest of tasks are to the success of the entire organization.

The more you master the details of your work, the more you'll realize that the building blocks you use to construct your success are exactly those details that you master along the way.

12

Upbuild Yourself And Others

I HIRED MOOSE CLEARY to frame houses for me in 1984. He was a longhaired guy who framed houses all day long. Boom, boom, boom, he'd pound the nails–every day for five, ten, fifteen years.

Moose was a hard worker, and I wanted to raise him up to the next level in his career.

"I like framing houses," he'd say. The next level would have put him in a position where he'd have to supervise others and deal with customers.

"I'm really happy doing what I'm doing."

I kept trying to get Moose up to the next level, but he kept refusing the additional responsibility. There was no question in my mind that he could handle it, but he wasn't as sure about himself as I was. Maybe he was scared of failure. Maybe he was scared of success.

Trying to get Moose up to the next level became a challenge for me. I kept on him. He was polite, but man, was he stubborn! Finally, I got him aside and said, "Look. You're ready for this. I need you to do this. You're getting older like me, and you need to put those tools down, Moose."

The words sunk in. Moose realized that if he didn't take advantage of the opportunity, he'd be sabotaging his future. So finally, he agreed to go for it.

I knew he was serious when he came into the office with a short haircut. It was a public symbol of his commitment to advancing his career.

Now Moose runs my entire framing division and takes all of our houses from foundation to framing inspection. His team has to get all the framing done, load all the roofing materials to see that each house can support the weight, and rough in all the plumbing and electrical systems. He's also responsible for buying all the lumber and other supplies necessary for his team to do its work.

Moose manages between 40 and 60 people, and has earned their love and respect. My customers feel the same way about him. But most importantly, Moose is enjoying the rewards that come from working hard, mastering the details, and moving up to the next level.

The cornerstone of my philosophy of hard work is a process my wife and I call upbuilding. I think it's a catchy way of saying that you should continually look for ways to advance your career.

Simply finding things to do and mastering the details can get stale if you keep doing the same things all the time. That's where upbuilding comes in. It's what makes the process of mastering the details dynamic.

To achieve real success, you have to keep doing both. You have to master the details in order to get the confidence to build yourself up to the next level. And when you get to the next level, you have to master a whole new set of details before you can move up again.

Upbuilding is the surest way I know to reach your goals and desires, and it's most effective after you've mastered the details of whatever level you're already on. Jump to the next level too early, and you put yourself at a greater risk of failure. Don't jump at all, and you deny your potential for success.

When you're ready to jump, how high do you go? We'll talk more specifically about goals in the next chapter, but for now I just want to say that I believe that many small jumps are more effective than a few big jumps. It's a lot easier to get to the top of the corporate ladder one step at a time. When you're upbuilding yourself, I think you should be very measured and deliberate about it. You only want to progress when you're ready, and you don't want to take on too much new responsibility at once. On the other hand, you don't want to let good opportunities pass you by. This could have easily happened to Moose.

Upbuilding requires risk, but it should be manageable risk. When you find yourself thinking about moving up to the next level in your career, first ask yourself if you've really mastered the details in your current situation. And second, decide how high to jump by weighing the risks of making the jump against the rewards of making it. It's an ongoing process, and the more you do it the easier it gets.

Mastering the details and upbuilding are the tools I used to build my entire career. I've said this before and I'm probably beating a dead horse here, but it's critical for you to understand how small steps can help you cover a tremendous amount of ground. When I got good at building two or three houses at a time, I raised the bar just the right amount by trying to build five houses at a time.

I may very well have been able to build twenty-five houses after mastering two or three, but that would have been too big a risk for me. Jumping to five houses at once seemed plenty challenging when I did it the first time, but it also felt doable, and I also felt that if I failed at it, I'd be able to regroup. Because building five houses was such a manageable progression, I had confidence in my ability to make it happen, and I was able to draw from my past experiences to get the results I wanted. Let me tell you, that's a much better way of approaching a job than questioning your abilities, stressing out about being in over your head, and freaking out about problems with no idea how to handle them.

I'll admit there were a couple of times when circumstances forced me to jump higher than I was comfortable jumping, and I was very fortunate that everything worked out in those situations. However, I believe that things worked out so well because, in all the previous circumstances over which I had control, I took a more conservative route. So, when I had to do something a little more risky, I already had a lot of good knowledge to back me up. I recommend taking a conservative approach to upbuilding when you can—especially early on. And, if and when you absolutely can't, pay close attention to your inner voice and trust your gut.

Like mastering the details, upbuilding engages you, involves you in your career, and puts you in charge of your destiny. If you're lucky enough to have a boss or a manager who wants you to reach your full potential, so much the better, but that's not necessary for you to start upbuilding yourself right away. The only person responsible for your continued improvement and ultimate success is you.

When you decide to upbuild yourself, you're motivated to work harder. Work becomes fun, interesting, exciting, and stimulating. Instead of seeing work as a waste of time or as just a way to help your boss succeed, work becomes an important investment of time and energy that can help *you* succeed.

When you upbuild yourself, you can look toward the future of your career with purpose, and you can look back on your career with great satisfaction. It's pretty powerful stuff!

Probably the best thing about upbuilding is that it works as long as you have the desire to learn, grow, and succeed.

Desire and enthusiasm are the key drivers of the upbuilding process. Mastering the details of what you're doing keeps that desire in check, and that's incredibly important. In my opinion, desire and enthusiasm alone can cause people to take bigger risks than they can handle. Desire and enthusiasm alone can cause people to jump too soon, before they're prepared. Desire and enthusiasm alone—without mastering the details—are probably responsible for more business failures than anything else.

Think about someone starting an exercise program—maybe this has even happened to you. If you do it right, you start slowly, work hard, and lift a little bit more weight every now and then without sacrificing your technique. After a few months or years of dedicated effort, you look like Arnold Schwarzenegger or my friend Clark Bartram, the fitness guru who's 40 years old and looks like he's 25.

If you're like most people, however, you get all excited, lift too much weight, and are so sore the next day that you can't even move. You get discouraged and never set foot in the gym again.

The same logic applies to careers. My advice is to take smaller steps than you think you should or could. Upbuilding requires a great deal of discipline—it's hard work in itself. It can be frustrating, especially if you're impatient and feel like everyone else is passing you by.

But believe me, if you take the time you need, raise the bar gradually, and work hard with a focus on doing your best and on enriching the lives of your co-workers and customers, you'll get closer to reaching your full potential. You may not get where you want to go as quickly as you want, but you're a lot more likely to get there at some point. When you upbuild yourself, you'll always be happy in your career, and yet you'll always want more at the same time. It's a dynamic tension that allows you to work hard in the moment and do a wonderful job, as well as build yourself up toward a bright and prosperous future.

While some people tend to jump too high too fast, others find it difficult to jump to higher levels of achievement and responsibility at all. Fear, guilt, and feelings of unworthiness can all put the brakes on the upbuilding process, or even prevent it from happening in the first place.

When done correctly, upbuilding takes away fear, guilt, and unworthiness. Because you make small improvements consistently over time, your confidence in your abilities remains high. And because you don't move up until you master the details of the level you're on, you feel like you really deserve to reach the higher levels.

Strange attitudes, beliefs, and feelings about money can also interfere with a person's career progress, but once again proper upbuilding takes care of the problem. Everyone says they want to be a millionaire, for example, but many people can't handle that kind of money, especially if they get it too quickly. You may not believe it, but Sudden Wealth Syndrome is a very real medical problem that's plagued many lottery winners and dot-com millionaires.

Some people think that it's difficult, or even impossible, to make a million dollars. Other people believe that millionaires are different from everybody else, or that too much money is evil, or that it's just a fun little fantasy to think about what to do with a million dollars. I don't mean to be flippant about it. Making a million dollars is something that a lot of people—even some hard workers—will never achieve. But I honestly believe that when you upbuild yourself in order to get it, it doesn't seem like such a big deal. By taking a slow and deliberate approach to success, upbuilding gradually prepares you for the wealth you're bound to earn when you follow the process of hard work that's outlined in this book. Upbuilding takes away emotional baggage about money by gradually getting people acquainted and comfortable with larger and larger bank accounts.

Upbuilding is great because it prevents the positive emotions of desire and enthusiasm from spinning out of control, and it keeps the negative emotions of fear, guilt, unworthiness, and uneasiness about money from sabotaging your success. Upbuilding, in its very logical, methodical way, really opens you up to the possibility of having more.

And once you start upbuilding, you never have to stop. I'm continually upbuilding myself and looking for new ways to succeed. I love my career and everything I've done to get where I am today, but at the same time I'm excited about the new directions I'll be going in tomorrow.

Writing this book has been a huge upbuilding experience for me. I never used to read at all. And now, much to the surprise and delight of my wife and kids, especially my daughter Ashley, I find myself going into bookstores every couple of weeks! I'm also hoping that this book will give me more opportunities to speak to people about the value of hard work and the methods I've used to maximize its effectiveness.

While upbuilding continues to help me achieve my individual career goals, it also serves me well as an effective management tool. Moose Cleary and Luis Feria are just two examples of how powerful upbuilding others can be for everyone concerned.

When it comes to co-workers, employees, or even bosses (sometimes they need upbuilding, too!), upbuilding means giving praise and offering people new challenges. Upbuilding is similar to mentoring, but it's not as formal or structured. In my mind, mentoring is more about getting somebody to be just like you, to follow in your footsteps, while upbuilding is more about helping individuals find the type of success that's right for them.

I don't think Moose, for example, wants to be Michael Crews, a developer, but he needed to do more than frame houses. I needed to help get him to the next level that was right for him, and I want to keep helping him get higher and higher—wherever he wants to go.

I never put a ceiling on the guys and gals who work with me. Moose can take his new job wherever he wants to take it. Right now, he's trying to get it all under his belt because he was strictly a framer before, a guy who knew nothing much other than how to put sticks up. All he did was pound nails and get those walls up, and boy, did he do it beautifully. He used his gifts and mastered all the details when it came to framing houses, but he got to a point where he was ready to move on. He was at the point of diminishing returns, and upbuilding allowed him to advance his career, achieve even more success, and use his years of experience to upbuild others.

Now Moose is mastering a whole new set of details, which make him nervous, excited, and motivated to win. He's been learning about plumbing, electrical, and mechanical systems. He's been learning about ordering supplies. He's been learning about managing people and being accountable when problems come up. He's a little bit out of his comfort zone, but he gains confidence because he has a history of mastering details and he has the full support of the Michael Crews Development team.

Whenever I see an employee with promise, like Moose, Luis, and countless others, I make a note to cultivate them and help them rise to their full potential. It's an activity that's both personally satisfying and professionally rewarding.

Upbuilding the people who work with me has been instrumental to my success. I need a team of great people to build so many perfect houses each year, and upbuilding assures me of three things—first, that I get the best work out of everyone involved; second, that I keep the best people for a long time; and third, that as people grow they'll upbuild others within the organization on their own.

It's all about being the best coach I can be for my team, and it requires timing on both sides. I can't force people to move up to the next level in their careers if they're not ready, and I risk losing some great people if I don't act quickly enough. At Michael Crews Development, we've been pretty good about upbuilding the people who work with us. Our turnover rate is extremely low, and many key people working with us today have been here from the very beginning.

I believe that upbuilding others is one of the most important skills a manager or business leader can have. Morale in the workplace goes up. People work harder and become more efficient, productive, and innovative. People stay with an organization and that continuity helps keep progress from being interrupted. And when new people join the company, right away they feel like they're in a safe, nurturing place filled with hard workers who want them to be star players, too. When a company adopts a culture that truly believes in the importance of upbuilding everyone within the entire enterprise, then quality goes up, employees and customers are happier, and sales increase.

Upbuilding is powerful stuff for any business. Try it on yourself, extend it to the people you work with, and watch the amazing results.

13

Set Goals You Can Reach

"I WANT TO SELL 52 new houses in 2000."

I made the announcement to my team at the Christmas party in 1999, and that's all anyone could talk about that night.

"That's an ambitious goal!" seemed to be the general consensus. Most people were excited about it and some people weren't too sure about it, but it got everyone energized. Even before January 2000, my team was strategizing.

Our rallying cry became "52-'N-52!" A house a week for 52 weeks.

Now, lots of builders build and sell more than 52 homes in a year, but we were building large, semi-custom homes on two-acre lots. We needed a lot of land, a lot of skilled craftsmen, and a lot of effective salespeople to reach our goal. We sold 41 houses the year before, so 52 houses was a little bit of a stretch for us. But it wasn't beyond the realm of possibility.

We did everything we could to make it happen. We made hats and T-shirts. We put up a big sign in the room where the Development Team has its weekly meetings, so everyone could see it. Underneath the big slogan we tracked our progress, much like my third-grade teacher did when I was trying to learn my multiplication tables (only now the technique works for me!).

Each week, we could see how we were doing. If we were on or ahead of our pace, we'd be excited, happy, and proud. If we were behind, we'd analyze the situation and figure out what we needed to do to get back on track.

By September, everyone was getting excited because it really looked as though we were going to make it. That made people work even harder.

It was amazing to watch the team come together around the goal. It created energy, enthusiasm, and lots of hard work.

And it paid off. In 2000, Michael Crews Development sold 52 houses.

Goals are roadmaps for upbuilding. When you master the details in your job and are ready to get to the next level in your career, you need to know where to go. You need to know where to direct your hard-work energy.

Most of my early career goals were targets, something to shoot at. When I started selling houses, my target was Tommy Hopkins's record of 10 straight Quota Buster Awards. I saw that the goal was attainable because someone else had already done it, and I wanted to do as well as he did, or better.

Now, as a business leader, I don't always have a point of reference as obvious as Tommy Hopkins's sales record. Because of this, my goals and the goals of my company are usually something to shoot for, rather than something to shoot at. We're continually breaking new ground with our goals, and these types of goals require some significant pre-planning.

When I establish an annual goal for my development business, I ask a lot of questions to figure out what goal makes the most sense. I want a goal that stretches me and my company, but I also want it to be realistic. How much land do we own? How much land can we obtain? Can our contractors increase their capacity to match our goals? If not, can we find additional contractors whose work we trust? Will the weather cooperate? Will the government add regulations that could slow our processes? Will we keep the same employees with the history behind them to stay strong and efficient?

The answers to these and other questions help me decide the best goals to set for Michael Crews Development each year. Some of the variables are within our control and others are not, but they all have to be factored in, using past experiences as a guide.

I've gotten pretty good at defining attainable goals for my company, and if we fall short it's usually because the weather is especially wet or the economy is especially depressed. When things like that happen, you have to be able to see the big picture and keep your goal setting on course. If I set a goal one year for 75 houses and we only sell 65 because of the weather, the economy, or a complicated new city permit process, I'd probably still set the next year's goal at 80 houses, or even higher.

If we only sold 65 houses because we just couldn't muster the hard work to do better, then I might keep the next year's goal at 75 houses. I never want to set a future goal lower than a current goal, unless we're selling a different type of house.

I believe that it's important to set goals as high as possible, but never so high that they demoralize my team. For groups as well as individuals, setting reasonable goals and committing to them completely is far better than setting bigger goals and getting discouraged. If you try as hard as you can and still don't reach a particular goal, you'll at least get closer to a smaller goal than you would to a bigger goal.

Setting goals you can reach allows you to push yourself, but it also minimizes your risk at the same time. You've probably noticed that minimizing risk is one of the central themes of my ideas about hard work. So far, all the steps we've talked about— finding something to do, using your gifts, mastering the details, and gradual upbuilding—have been about achieving success by minimizing your risk. It's the same with goals. If you set your sights on smaller goals, you'll be able to focus more of your energy on working hard to reach them, instead of worrying about being in way over your head. And if you do fall short, you'll be in a better position to analyze what happened, refocus, and start tackling your next goal with knowledge and enthusiasm.

When I started building houses, my goals were conservative. Build one house. Build one house again. Build two houses. Build three houses. Build five houses. Build ten houses. I stretched myself with each goal, but not to the point where I couldn't realistically achieve the goal, or to the point where failure to achieve the goal would have bankrupted my business.

Setting goals you can reach gives you confidence in your abilities. When I was in the early stages of my career, I needed the small successes to gain confidence, and I needed the detailed knowledge of the smaller projects to successfully accomplish bigger things in the future. Patience is a virtue.

Today, as the manager of a team, I know that I have a good goal when about two-thirds of the people I tell think it's ambitious but doable, and the other third thinks it's next to impossible.

Skeptics are important when you're setting goals, but you don't want too many of them. You want people to voice objections to your goals because then you can discuss potential problems and come up with strategies to deal with them in advance. Objections can also fire up your competitive spirit and give you extra motivation to prove the skeptics wrong. After objections are raised, heard, and talked about, a good team rallies around the goal and does what it takes to achieve it.

When your goal is just at the edge of where the possible meets the impossible, it creates an amazing energy that generates a lot of hard work. To keep this energy up, I recommend making your goal public and writing it down so that you and anyone else involved in helping you achieve the goal can see it on a regular basis. Making a goal public makes it real. It makes you accountable. It motivates you to succeed.

I announced that I was going to write this book at one of my Development Team meetings. As expected, I got a mixed response. About two-thirds of my team thought it was great, ambitious, and exciting, and the other third thought I was crazy. "You can't even *read* books, Mike!" they'd say, half-joking.

It was good to hear this kind of skepticism, because it gave me more of a reason to succeed—I had to prove them wrong! It was important for me to publicly go out on a limb and hear the objections out loud in order to spark the energy I needed to succeed.

Until I told my staff that I was writing this book, I was never compelled to actually figure out what I needed to do to make it happen. Writing the book was something I wanted to do, but making it public turned it into something I had to do. When I say I'm going to do something, I mean it. So announcing this project to the group made me accountable for its becoming a reality and gave me a stake in making it a success.

When you go public with a goal, you're simply more likely to achieve it. The big sign we put up in our meeting room with our annual sales goal on it acts as a constant reminder of what we believe we're capable of if we work hard and push ourselves to the next levels of efficiency, productivity, and creativity.

When a guy on the framing crew wears his T-shirt with our current goal on it, he reinforces his commitment to its success and reminds the rest of the team that we're on a mission. Even when someone on our team wears a T-shirt from a previous year, it reminds us of our ability to achieve goals. (I have to tell you, our guys and gals have a pretty goal-oriented wardrobe.)

And similarly, when someone who reads my quarterly newsletter sees me on the street and asks me in July if I'm halfway to my annual sales goal yet, it forces me to think about where we are and what we need to do to stay, or get back, on track. These little public reminders constantly inspire us to succeed, or to at least get as close to achieving our goals as we possibly can.

In 2001, our goal was 72 houses for the year. We only sold 47 houses during that calendar year, and we learned the hard way that hard work and public declarations alone do not guarantee goal achievement. The horrifying events of 9/11 had a huge impact on our business—we were basically shut down for two months. And earlier that year, Valley Center had one of the wettest springs in recent history. Every day it rained, we had to delay or halt construction. With all this working against us, we struggled against our goal of 72 houses. We finally achieved it in 2002, while we were simultaneously working on new goals for the new year as well.

As I said before, variables outside your control shouldn't dampen your enthusiasm, as long as you're doing your best and working your hardest. Despite a disappointing 2001, my team members learned a great deal about each other, we became stronger and even more efficient in our jobs, and we grew a lot closer together. The setbacks of 2001 actually served to build even greater camaraderie around the office, and, as bad as it was, the experience actually prepared us for greater accomplishments in the future. In 2003, I set our annual goal at 100 houses.

It seemed like too big a jump to some people, but when I analyzed the situation, looked at how we developed as a team because of the problems we faced, and answered all my usual questions, 100 houses seemed like a reasonable amount for 2003.

As I write these words, I'm confident that we're going to reach our goal. We have enough land, my construction crews are wowing me every day, and my sales team keeps closing deal after deal. There's such a great energy here these days, and people are working harder than I've ever seen. Plus, we're all getting an extra push from the fact that we have the opportunity to break into triple-digits. I have to tell you, it's pretty exciting around Michael Crews Development these days!

I've talked a lot about my goals in this chapter, but this book is really about you and your goals in the business world. I hope my stories have illustrated the idea that it's better to make smaller goals you can achieve than it is to make bigger goals that have a greater risk of failure. In the long run, you'll get farther a lot faster if you take a more conservative approach.

You'll probably have many goals in place at the same time. That's great, and it gives you even more of a reason to write your goals down on paper and make them public—just to help you keep track of them all.

I like to think in terms of short-term goals, mid-term goals, and long-term goals. Short-term goals might be as simple as finishing a report a day before it's due, making three sales calls each day, reading a good business book, or cleaning your desk and organizing your files. Mid-term goals can be things you want to achieve in one month to one year, such as taking a training class or successfully completing a big project. My annual sales goals, for example, are mid-term goals. Long-term goals are things you want to achieve in more than one year. Your long-term goals might include getting a promotion, making a certain salary, or starting your own business.

Obviously, you'll need to come up with your own goals based on your desires and the realities of your current situation. When you do this, organize your goals by time, see which ones need to be accomplished before others, and think about how they overlap and work together. A little planning will make it easier for you to make sure that everything you do gets you closer to achieving your goals.

And then there are dreams. Big, wonderful dreams. Without big dreams, all goals are meaningless.

Big dreams are at the heart of any success story. My big dream was to make something of myself in my community, and having that with me every step of the way propelled me to keep moving forward.

What's your big dream? Financial freedom? Owning your own business? Sending your kids to college? Retiring at age 45? Being a vice president of your company? Think about it for awhile and come up with something as big as you can believe in.

A big dream is your personal vision for your perfect future. I talk a lot about vision and focus in this book, and it's important that you understand how these two things are different and how they work together. If your big dream is your overall vision for how you want your life to look, each little goal you set along the way is where you need to focus your attention if you ultimately want to realize your vision.

By focusing on each goal—no matter how insignificant it seems compared to your overall dream—and by mastering the details before moving on to the next goal, you get closer and closer to your vision of success through the process of upbuilding. It may not always feel exciting, and you may often find yourself on a long plateau, but over time the technique is effective. If you're persistent and patient, there's really nothing you can't achieve.

Having a big dream to reach for gives you the energy and motivation you need to spark yourself into action. But it's the consistent achievement of smaller goals over time that sustains that energy and allows you to eventually reach that big dream.

Before I retire, my goal is to build 150 houses like the ones we're building today on two-acre lots in one year. Twenty years ago, that would have seemed like a total fantasy. But now it seems possible. Now it seems that, at some point, we'll make it happen. I'm not going to attempt it next year or the year after that. I'm not in a hurry, but I know that each year brings me a little more knowledge and a little more confidence. Each year brings me closer to that particular dream. And knowing me, by the time I build 150 houses in one year, I'll have my sights set on building 200!

All of the actions we've discussed so far that can help you achieve success through hard work are dependent upon goals. When you find something to do, you automatically set goals because you're motivated to achieve. When you decide to use your gifts, you set goals that are enjoyable to reach for. When you master the details, you focus on doing the things you need to do in order to get closer to achieving your goals. And when you upbuild yourself and others, you keep looking for new goals that are within reach. Through setting and achieving goals, the hard-work actions we've discussed so far have the power to give you amazing amounts of confidence, knowledge, skill, success, and joy in your career.

Keep your goals realistic, but keep your dreams big. Give every goal your best shot. And by all means celebrate and learn from your achievements, whether you reach all your goals or not.

14

Be Creative

I SAW THE "FOR SALE BY OWNER" SIGN
one Sunday while I was driving home after church.

It was in front of a little green dollhouse that was built in the 1940s on a beautiful tree-lined street in an older section of Escondido, California. I fell in love with that house on the spot.

Ever since I graduated from high school, it was an urgent goal of mine to purchase a house. As far as I was concerned, every day that I didn't own a house was a day I was wasting money by renting an apartment. I was 19 years old when I drove past the little green dollhouse.

Then I saw the man painting.

I parked the car, got out, and introduced myself to the man, who turned out to be the owner of the house.

"My name's Mr. Good," he said.

"Well," I replied. "If you want to do something good today, you'll sell me your house."

"Can you afford it?" he asked. He wanted $29,000.

"I don't have a lot of money," I said. At that time, I was still working at the water company.

"Do you have a job?"

"Yeah," I replied. "Lots of them!"

We talked for awhile and I told him about my jobs, about growing up in Escondido, and about how I wanted to make something of my life.

"You seem like a nice young man," he said, sizing me up. "How much do you have for a down payment?"

"I have $3,000."

"I'll tell you what I'm going to do," Mr. Good said. "Give me your $3,000 and I'll be the bank on this deal. You pay me $200 every month and the house is yours."

Two hundred dollars a month was a lot of money for me back then—I really had to dig deep to make the payments. But it was less than a bank would have charged me—assuming I could have qualified for a loan—so I decided to go for it.

"Thanks, Mr. Good," I said, smiling from ear to ear as we shook hands on the deal.

———

When people tell me there's no way, I have a problem with that. If there's a will, there's always a way. Always.

Creativity is the mental force that allows you to reach your goals and dreams, no matter what obstacles are stacked against you. Creativity allows you to get what you want through unconventional methods, even when you don't seem to have the necessary resources like money, an education, or the right connections.

Creativity is a necessary element of effective hard work, just like finding something to do, using your gifts, mastering the details, and setting goals you can achieve.

I like to think of creativity as the mother of good luck—a magical force that you can access when you need it to get out of a jam or solve a really tough problem. When all your careful planning goes wrong, creativity is the power that can save you. When we were building Orange Glen Estates, Hidden Valley Homes, and Hidden Valley Homes II (and found ourselves overextended with three expensive properties), creativity got us out of a potentially disastrous situation. Asking the bank if they'd take less money for the foreclosure property if we paid in cash and petitioning the city to change the zoning for Hidden Valley Homes II were two creative ideas that solved our cash flow problems. Creativity doesn't have to be outrageously funny or clever, it just has to be smart and effective.

Now, I know exactly what you're thinking: "I'm not creative or lucky." In my opinion, that just means you don't realize how much control the focused hard worker has over luck and creativity. You don't realize yet how making a commitment to working hard can lead you directly toward creative solutions and lucky breaks.

Creativity and luck are valuable tools of the hard worker who's committed to goals and dreams, especially when those goals and dreams are written down, made public, and constantly looked at.

When you have a big overall vision and can focus your attention on achieving goals that allow you to make that vision a reality, you naturally begin to look at things from new and different angles. You start seeing opportunities where there weren't any before. You open your mind to approaching things in unconventional ways.

I believe that when you commit to a goal and keep an open mind, creative solutions appear to you. When I was 19 years old, Mr. Good showed me that I could reach my goal of buying a house in a creative way. If I had thought only conventionally, it could have taken me years to get my own house.

The same thing is true about how I found a house to put on the first piece of investment property I bought. If I wasn't open to creative opportunities, I would never have noticed the ad for the auction, I never would have gotten a house for only $500, and I certainly never would have been able to figure out how to move the house onto my property.

I never had many of the traditional resources that people think they need to be successful. I didn't start out with a lot of money, and I didn't have a fancy degree. All I had was my commitment to my goals and the good sense to know that there's more than one way to skin a cat.

Never use a perceived lack of resources as an excuse for not being a success. That's a cop out. There are too many examples of people who started out with nothing and made it big to allow an excuse like that to hold water. Use creativity to bring you the resources you need to reach your goals.

When I talk with people who want to get ahead, I always tell them to buy real estate. I think it's a great investment, and I think it also gives people a way to experience the joys of hard work. It's certainly worked for me, so I constantly tell people to buy some property and rent it out. The biggest objection I get when I give this advice is that the person can't afford it. Okay, so be creative. As I tell the college kids I talk to, go in on something as a group. If you go into a deal with four other people, you still have 20% ownership of a piece of property, and that's better than where you're at now. Then, if you sell the property in a few years, maybe you'll have enough money to own 50% of a new piece of property.

Creativity, along with the deliberate process of continually upbuilding yourself, is one powerful force.

The best thing about creativity is that it doesn't cost anything, and it's available in unlimited amounts to anyone who wants to use it. As a business resource, it's pure gold.

Everyone on this planet has the potential to be creative. All you have to do to tap into the power of creativity is be open to it, watch for it, believe that it'll come when you need it, and embrace it when it does. If you can do that, incredible opportunities and innovative solutions will present themselves to you on a regular basis.

15

Hold Yourself Accountable

I'VE SOLD THOUSANDS OF HOUSES, but I own every one of them.

I don't really own them, my customers do.

But I do own all the work that goes into building each house produced by Michael Crews Development. I also own any problems that occur as a result of that work.

My name is on every house we build–literally. In the bottom corner of the window next to the front door of each completed house, we etch a small Michael Crews Development logo.

It's a signature, and I put it on our houses just as an artist puts his or her signature on a painting.

It tells my customers that I'm proud of my team's hard work, and that I'm willing to be held accountable for anything that might go wrong as a result of our efforts to build a quality home.

Accountability is all about ownership. It's about owning your job, owning your career, and owning your successes and failures.

Accountability is about doing the best job you can do, and accepting responsibility for any mistakes you might make along the way. Accountability is also about fully completing any job or task that you take on, no matter how difficult, complicated, or crazy it gets.

Accountability is about integrity. It's about character. It's about building trust, even if you're not always perfect.

It's not always fun to be accountable for your actions, but it goes a long way toward bringing you the kind of success you really desire.

I don't know if there's any way to learn how to be accountable. It's one of those things that you just have to start doing. Like creativity, its power is there for the taking, free of charge.

I was lucky enough to have been accountable for my actions starting at a very young age. My mom recently told me that all the other parents of kids in my high school would only let their kids go to various parties and social events if they knew I was going with them! They knew that if I was around, their kids wouldn't get into any trouble.

Today, people seem almost embarrassed to have integrity or to be honest and accountable for their actions. Being accountable isn't cool. It's not hip. It's only for suckers who are too stupid to know that they're being taken advantage of.

I find this tremendously sad, because a lack of accountability affects all aspects of people's lives. If someone refuses to be accountable at work or at school, how can they be accountable at home?

In business, many people think that the way to get ahead is by *not* being accountable. These people believe that the people who get to the top are the crafty, deceitful ones who step over everyone else on their way up the ladder. Honest people are pushovers. Nice guys finish last.

Well, that's not the way it works in my world. From where I sit, the people who hold themselves accountable are ultimately the most successful ones. In my experience, the people who aren't accountable can expect to face one of three undesirable fates. First, those who are obviously unaccountable don't even get a chance. They're always getting fired, and drift from job to job without ever getting ahead. Second, those who do fool people and rise up the ladder tend to fall harder the higher up they go. And third, those few who slip through the cracks and never get caught still have to live with themselves.

On the other hand, people who are accountable for their work reap lots of positive rewards that lead to joyful, successful careers. When you hold yourself accountable for your work, your interactions with your co-workers are less stressful. There's more love, camaraderie, and respect in the work environment, and less anger, fear, fatigue, and frustration.

When you hold yourself accountable for your work, you don't have to be afraid of making a mistake. Everyone will know that if you do make a mistake, you'll make it right. You don't have to get mad at criticism. You know that your work is a learning experience and you'll want to keep learning and getting better. Most people who hold themselves accountable don't even get yelled at in the first place, and if something does go wrong they have a calm discussion about it with their boss and figure out a solution. And when you hold yourself accountable for your work, you don't have to waste your time criticizing others. You're too busy looking for ways that you could have made the situation better, and too busy working on the only person you have any control over—yourself.

If you deal directly with customers, being accountable helps those relationships, too. When you hold yourself accountable, you can look your customers in the eye, knowing that you've done the best you can to make them happy. You can field every complaint with a sincere resolve to correct the problem—for the customer who's complaining and every customer who comes after him.

I'm in a rather unique position when it comes to customers, because I see mine all the time. I see my customers every day at the post office, at the grocery store, at the mall, and at my favorite restaurants. I run into them on the street. They know where I live. I know where they live. Many of my customers are people I buy things from and deal with on a regular basis.

Because I'm accountable for my work, these chance meetings with my customers are always enjoyable and pleasant. They're never awkward, tense, or embarrassing in any way. Usually, when I run into customers in town, they tell me how happy they are with their houses. On the rare occasions when someone does have a question or a problem, they know they can talk to me about it honestly and openly without my getting defensive.

When you're accountable for your actions in the business world, you develop trust among all the people you do business with. And let me tell you, trust goes a long way when you need people to help you get ahead.

In the development business, we rely on bankers to finance the projects we want to build. In the early days, the bankers in my area didn't know anything about Michael Crews or Art Duncan. But they did know Darryl Duncan, Art's dad.

Art and I both worked for Mr. Duncan when we were in high school. He knew first-hand that we were hard workers who held ourselves accountable for our work. He also saw how accountable we were when we figured out how to move a house onto the lot I owned, fix it up, and sell it for a profit. He trusted us to do the right thing, and that's why he introduced us to his bankers. His bankers trusted him, and that's why they agreed to do business with us.

But it didn't stop there. You can never stop being accountable. I've already told you the story of Silver Oaks, where I paid the bank first even though the economy was bad and the project barely made any money. That's what being accountable is all about, and that's how it helps you get ahead.

Because of my consistent accountability, I was able to get to the point where the bankers I work with are more concerned with me than with the reasons I want to borrow their money. I could probably get financing for the most outlandish scheme in the world, because the banks know that I'll pay them back first no matter what happens.

The beauty of being accountable is that it makes you do the right thing. Holding yourself accountable prevents you from taking shortcuts. It prevents you from stealing and cheating. It prevents you from lying. It prevents you from all the negative behaviors that give business a bad name and a reputation for being corrupt.

Holding yourself accountable is yet another action that gives you the energy you need to work hard so you can do quality work that enriches the lives of your co-workers and customers.

Like every other hard-work action we've discussed so far, holding yourself accountable engages you in your job. By owning your work, you take pride in your work. Holding yourself accountable gives you the motivation you need to master the details and find creative solutions, and it gives you the confidence you need to set higher and higher goals for yourself.

Holding yourself accountable is not always an easy thing to do, especially when others around you aren't accountable for their actions, but it will serve you well in your quest for success.

16

Relax And See The Big Picture

WORMS TAUGHT ME A BIG LESSON when I was 17 years old–regular, garden-variety earthworms.

Worms were big business in my town back then. They were easy to raise, and you could sell them for fishing, gardening, and all kinds of other things.

My dad and I talked about getting into the worm business together, but I wanted to do it all myself.

"We could be partners," my dad said.

"No, dad. This one's all mine."

I scraped up $400 on my own and was ready to get to work. It was a real no-brainer. All you had to do was buy the first batch of worms, put them in a ten-foot-by-three-foot wooden box with some fertilizer, and water them every few days. Do this and your worm business was guaranteed to naturally double every 60 days.

Talk about a sure thing!

I started my worm business with great enthusiasm and a lot of desire. I built the wooden boxes, shoveled out rabbit cages to get free fertilizer, and watched my business grow. For six months, everything was going great, and I had eight long boxes of worms going strong in the backyard.

But then, I lost everything.

I didn't water the worms for a few days, and they just dried up.

It was my own fault. My girlfriend, my other jobs, and sports distracted me. I soon realized that my refusal to cut my dad in the business was a big mistake.

I got mad. I got mad about losing my investment and all the potential income from my growing business. I got mad about wasting all that time shoveling out rabbit cages. I got mad at my dad for not insisting to be partners. And I got mad at myself, because work was the one thing I was supposed to be really good at.

But getting mad didn't change the fact that my worm business dried up–literally. Eventually, I calmed down. I even learned a valuable lesson: If you want to succeed in business, you've got to water your worms!

I tell my worm story to illustrate the fact that long-term success allows for short-term failures as long as you handle them well and turn them into positive learning experiences. While you may stumble, your overall success as a hard worker is virtually guaranteed if you relax and see the big picture. My short stint as a worm rancher taught me the importance of focus, and every job I've taken ever since then has had my undivided attention.

My failure in the worm business was my own fault. I had no one to blame but myself. That can be difficult to accept sometimes, but when you're accountable for your work, you own up to your failures and learn from them.

It can be even harder to relax and see the big picture when you do everything right and still run into problems. On a flight to Texas, my partner Art sat next to a man who started telling him about the profits he could make in the ostrich business. The guy got Art all fired up, and when Art came back to Valley Center he convinced me, and a guy named Mike Zajda, to start a business we called Valley-Tex Farms.

Art and I each put in $50,000. Mike was in charge of the day-to-day operations of the farm, which he ran out of his backyard. We purchased a mom ostrich and a dad ostrich, and Mike built an impressive incubation room where we could hatch the eggs.

We got a little impatient with the two adult ostriches, who weren't producing eggs fast enough. So we decided to buy some eggs from other farms. I remember flying around in my small plane to get these ostrich eggs that cost $1,500 each. Talk about precious cargo! We had to carefully place the eggs in boxes filled with birdseed to prevent them from cracking in transit.

The strategy, and our hard work, began to pay off. Before too long, we had about 40 little ostrich babies running around in a pen that Mike had built. Our high-protein herd was growing, and we were getting ready to take orders!

One day, however, Mike noticed that one of the baby ostriches was walking kind of funny. Art and I came over to take a look, and sure enough this one little ostrich was zigzagging around like a drunken bum. A short while later, the poor thing collapsed and died. Before the veterinarian could come to the farm, another baby ostrich met the same fate. After two weeks, all of our ostriches had died from a viral disease that no amount of hard work could have overcome.

Our dreams of being ostrich tycoons were shattered, even though we did everything right. We mastered the details of the incubation process. We used creativity to get more ostrich eggs.

We started small and set achievable goals. But in the end, there were no profits. There was only a valuable learning experience.

What I learned from the ostrich business is that anger is really pointless when setbacks occur, whether circumstances are in your control or not. Anger doesn't change the situation. It doesn't bring the ostriches back. All anger does is waste your time and give you a reason to prevent yourself from being successful.

I truly believe that how a person deals with problems is the true measure of their success. Successful people understand the ultimate insignificance of individual problems and move on, while unsuccessful people tend to give up when problems arise.

My philosophy is never to let a problem get the best of me. I've found that it serves me better in the long run not to get mad, whether a problem is caused by me, someone else, or another variable completely out of anyone's control.

If I make a mistake, I can learn from it. I can analyze what I did and do better next time. If someone I work with makes a mistake, I can learn from that, too. I can look inside myself and see if I gave that person the resources he or she needed to succeed. Or I can talk to the person about what happened and come up with better strategies for future projects. I can say, "Look, you're in charge of this and I'm counting on you to make sure you check this. Let's forget about it now, but next time make sure you check it." And if a problem occurs because of an act of God or another variable that I have no control over, then where do I even begin to direct my anger?

Don't get me wrong, I often get disappointed and upset when problems occur, but I work through it and quickly move on. I try to relax so creative solutions can present themselves, and I try to see the big picture that makes each individual problem seem insignificant. Rather than dwell on a problem, make a mountain out of a molehill, and stew in my anger, the more productive solution is to turn my hard-work switch back on and regroup.

Not getting mad is one of the hardest things you're going to have to deal with as you upbuild your career, but like all the other actions I've outlined in the hard-work process, it's necessary if you truly want to be successful.

I use five techniques to keep anger from getting in the way of my business. The first is to address problems directly, as soon as they occur. This channels your anger energy into something productive and ties into the idea of being accountable. It also has another benefit if the problem affects someone else, like a customer. If they can see that you're addressing their problem and trying to make things right, they're usually more relaxed about the whole thing, too.

If one of my customers has a problem, I want the problem fixed within 48 hours. Emergencies are handled sooner than that. No one at Michael Crews Development wants to have customer service issues hanging out there. For one thing, they distract us from our main job of building houses, and secondly, they just aren't good for people. We can analyze the situation later, but the first order of business is to fix whatever the problem is. If complaints don't get handled quickly, they can turn into monumental problems that can lead to lawsuits. Out of 2,500 homes, we've never had an insurance claim. This is very rare in the development business, and it's because we make customer service such a big priority.

Many people believe that if you ignore a problem it'll go away, but in reality the problem just gets bigger. Dealing with a problem takes time and can cost money, but the sooner you address it the more you can minimize its impact on your bottom line. A problem should take top priority because it's like a disease that can impact the health of your business, and you want it out of the system so it doesn't spread.

When you're addressing problems that involve other people, be sure to talk with those people in person. If you can't meet with them, talk to them over the phone. Yes, it can be uncomfortable sometimes, but hiding behind a fax or an e-mail when personal contact would be more appropriate just makes things worse in the long run. If I hide behind a problem, I still have a problem. But if I solve a problem, it's done and I can move on.

We get so much repeat business and so many referrals at Michael Crews Development because we address problems right away. We're on them immediately. As soon as we understand the issue, we figure out a strategy, talk to all the people involved, and go after it.

The second technique I use to keep myself from getting mad is to simply expect problems and mistakes as a cost of doing business. While I want everything my team does to be perfect, I never plan on everything going perfectly. By factoring in problems and planning for them in advance, you give yourself some breathing room when they occur. And if things do go perfectly, then you're pleasantly surprised.

It's difficult to give you any specific advice about planning for problems because I don't know your particular situation, but I can give you some examples. If you're working on a project that has a budget, for instance, add 3% as a contingency fund. If you're working on a deadline, make your deadline a day or two early so you have some "extra" time to fix things. If you're preparing a report, build in some time to have someone else review it—a fresh set of eyes is one of the best ways to catch mistakes.

Too often, people don't account for problems. They expect everything to go perfectly, and when it doesn't, they get upset. Then all they can see is the failed result, and they get stuck in anger mode. If you expect things to go a little less than perfect from the beginning, you give yourself a buffer zone that lets you keep your cool when problems occur.

I consider myself lucky to be in a business that's noted for problems, because I have to expect that they're going to happen. If you ever get two builders in the same room, inevitably the talk will turn to horror stories about who's had the biggest problems.

Knowing that problems are going to be a regular cost of doing business leads into the third technique I use to keep myself from getting angry about work—making problems positive. People who can make lemonade out of lemons have a huge capacity for success in their lives.

Sometimes, failures lead to incredibly wild successes. If I'm not mistaken, Post-it Notes and corn flakes were both "problems" that turned into valuable products. Now, maybe your mistakes and problems won't lend themselves to such dramatic turn-arounds, but every cloud has a silver lining.

At minimum, I always try to learn from my problems. Since they're a cost of doing business, I figure that at least I'm buying a valuable learning experience when a problem arises. Sometimes it's as simple as learning how not to make the same mistake twice. If it's more complicated than that, take the time to really analyze the situation and figure out what went wrong. Simply getting mad and blaming other people or events won't give you any useful information you can use if a similar problem presents itself in the future.

In addition to providing learning experiences, another positive feature of problems is the increased camaraderie they can create. When my team fell short of our annual development goal in 2001, our ability to rally in the face of problems actually allowed us to become a stronger team. Our struggle against a goal that was ultimately too big for us brought everyone closer together, so a lot of good came out of that particular failure. We were able to pull ourselves together the following year and tackle a new goal that was even more ambitious.

The fourth anger-management technique I use at work is to do my best to minimize problems in the first place. By mastering the details of a particular task and by doing that task repeatedly over time, you can avoid more and more problems as you get more skilled.

You can also prevent problems, or at least catch them as early as possible, by having open communication with your team at all times. At Michael Crews Development, we have weekly Development Team meetings at which everyone talks about everything they're doing on current projects. We do the same thing each week with the Engineering Team, only then we talk about our future projects. Touching base with the people you work with on a regular basis is a great way to head off problems and stay on track, but it's important to understand that there's never a bad time to talk when it comes to avoiding problems.

I rely on everyone on my team to contact me, or their direct manager, immediately if they ever notice a problem on a job site. It happens all the time. And, believe me, when a guy calls me on his cell phone and says, "Hey, I just left lot 46 and I saw a leak in the plumbing"—and we can get in there and fix it before it becomes a disaster—that's going to save our business a lot of money.

I would guess that more problems are caused by a lack of communication than any other reason. So start talking to the people you work with. If you have questions, ask them. If you have comments, don't keep them to yourself. If you make a mistake or notice something wrong, tell someone. It may feel uncomfortable, but it will be appreciated in the long run.

Accountability is another factor that helps you minimize problems. At my company, we make our accountability official by signing off on our work at key points. When the dirt is ready, the grading crew signs off on their work. When the framing is done, same thing. Every time one of our houses reaches an important milestone, everything done up to that point is accounted for and documented.

The fifth thing I do to keep from getting mad in business is probably the most important. It's to always count my blessings. I have my health, I have a strong faith, I have a great family, I have wonderful friends, and I've had lots of successes. A work problem would have to be pretty big to overshadow all of that!

I remind myself each day how lucky I am to even be alive. I remind myself that I have a lot going for me, no matter how many problems I face. I remind myself how problems can only make me stronger and bring more blessings into my life if I have the courage to deal with them, take responsibility for them, and learn from them. And I remind myself that getting mad is a big waste of time and energy that could be spent on hard work.

Avoiding anger helps you stay relaxed, so you can see how your work fits into the big picture of your life. It's interesting, but when you see the big picture of your job, you're able to understand the seeming contradiction that while work is only part of what makes you a person, it is at the same time much larger than your life.

When we work, we never work alone. Every person's work touches other people, from co-workers and outside suppliers to customers. My doing this book has had, and will continue to have, an impact on everyone in my company and everyone in my family, and the hard work has extended to designers, photographers, publishers, printers, marketers, public relations people, book reviewers, distributors, librarians, bookstore owners, and readers like you.

No matter what you do for a living, the physical act of going to work each day has an impact on many other real, live, breathing, thinking human beings who have jobs, families, problems, goals, and dreams of their own.

This probably isn't news to anybody, but how many people do you know at your place of business who keep these big-picture ideas top of mind? In my experience, most of the people who participate in "the daily grind"—the people who are the unhappiest about their careers—don't concern themselves much with the big picture. They tend to take a narrow view of their work and are only concerned with how their jobs affect themselves as individuals. They focus on their own comfort. They focus on how much money they're making or not making. They focus on how late they can arrive in the morning and how soon they can leave in the evening without getting into trouble. Work loses all meaning and joy for these people, and it becomes a chore that they do resentfully in return for paychecks they don't appreciate.

I'm not saying that personal needs and concerns aren't important at work. Not at all. Hard workers think about their own needs all the time, but they go beyond them and recognize that their work—whatever it is—has value to others in addition to themselves.

To the hard worker, work can be almost spiritual, almost sacred. It's been said that work is love made visible. There's a great deal of truth to that statement. I believe that work is more enjoyable, engaging, interesting, and fun when you realize that your job connects you to your co-workers, your customers, and yes, even to the rest of humanity.

For me, seeing the big picture makes it easier to do any job well. There's an element of pride in this, which gives you a genuine satisfaction in knowing that doing the best you can at your job is helping other people. This is why I had so much trouble selling Kirby vacuum cleaners. I did a good job and worked really hard, but I wasn't proud of it because I didn't believe I was helping anybody. Maybe I could have seen it differently, but at the time I was sick to my stomach and felt miserable whenever I had to go pick up one of the vacuum cleaners I "sold" and refund the customer's money.

I've felt great about every other job I've had. When I was delivering water tanks, I really felt like I was providing a valuable service for the customers of Rayne Water Conditioning. It made me happy, even though my back was breaking and I only made $2.80 an hour. When I sold houses to first-time home buyers who normally wouldn't have even considered buying a house, I felt like I was fulfilling a purpose much larger than the money I was getting. And today, when I build the best house I can possibly build and get letters of thanks and praise from my customers, that in itself fills me with great pride and love for the work I do.

Seeing the big picture is a skill that's difficult for people today. We all want instant gratification. We all want to be better than everyone else. And we all think that if we look at the big picture we're just going to be taken advantage of. This is so funny to me because seeing the big picture is really the surest way to get instant gratification, to be the best at what you do, and to prevent yourself from being taken advantage of. If you can see the truth in this, then you're well on your way to a successful career.

I've always built my business with the idea that I'm going to be around for a long time. I want my co-workers and customers to feel like my business is going to be around for a long time, too, so they can focus on their jobs and feel good about their purchases.

I treat my co-workers and customers right because I see the big picture. I see that it benefits me and everybody else in my organization. If you treat people right, it always comes back to you tenfold.

Many companies today sentence themselves to death by missing the big picture. They think they'll save money if they put restrictions on their employees, force workers to hit sales targets and call them on the carpet if they fall short, and implement complicated performance reviews that instill fear in individuals and destroy morale among teams.

These companies miss out on the powerful impact that basic decency, respect, and love could have on their productivity and efficiency. Instead, they waste their energy with numbers, charts, graphs, and quotas and forget that work is done by human beings.

When you relax and see the big picture, you're less likely to complain about your job or get angry at problems, and are more likely to think of positive ways to make your job better for yourself, your co-workers, and the customers of your business. Relaxing and seeing the big picture helps make work a joyful activity that you can commit to totally, instead of something that fills you with irritation and frustration.

17

Be A Hands-On Leader

"WHAT A WONDERFUL EVENING," Kelly said as she leaned over to give me a kiss.

I wanted to do something really special for this beautiful woman who was introduced to me by some mutual friends.

So that night, I picked her up and flew her to Vegas. We had dinner, caught a show, and spent the whole night on the town. By the time we flew back and I dropped her off at her house, it was three o'clock in the morning

I was pretty tired, but I had work to do. I was in the middle of the Silver Oaks project, the development I decided to go ahead with despite tough economic times in North County.

One of the ways developers market their projects is by putting up what's known in the trade as bootleg signs. Bootleg signs are those cardboard posters stapled on wooden stakes that you see by the side of the road, pointing people to different developments. "Turn Right To

New Homes" one sign might say, while another may read, "Luxury Homes Ahead Two Miles."

Developers put these signs up early on Saturday mornings. The signs have to come down by Sunday night. For Silver Oaks, we had to put up and take down about 150 signs each week.

The budget for Silver Oaks was so tight that we couldn't afford to hire any extra people to put up and take down our bootleg signs. The responsibility fell squarely on the shoulders of my sales director, Nick Antonocci.

Now, you've got to understand that putting up and taking down bootleg signs is a tough job. You have to use a sledgehammer to get the wooden stakes in the ground, you have to use a staple gun to secure the signs on the stakes, you have to work in the middle of the night, and every now and then someone throws an orange or an egg at you from their car. I couldn't ask Nick to do all that work himself.

As a hands-on leader, I offered to do it with him.

For at least two years, I spent two and a half hours every Saturday morning putting up bootleg signs and one and a half hours every Sunday night taking them down. It wasn't much fun, but it was something I had to do.

My pager went off at about ten o'clock in the morning. It was a text message from Kelly. "I don't know if you're up yet," she wrote, "but I wanted to thank you for last night."

I called her back right away. "Up yet!" I exclaimed. "I haven't even gone to bed!"

━━━━━━━━━

The best way to lead, in my opinion, is to get your hands dirty.

Michael Crews Development runs 100% from the top down. I'm never too good to get into the trenches with my guys and gals. I'm never too good to work with the salespeople and help them sell houses. And I'm never too good to pick up the trash in the office or around a job site.

I built my business by doing all these tasks myself, so I have a real appreciation for everything that goes into improving a piece of land, building a house on it, and selling the results. Why would I deny myself the chance to use my experience to help the people who work with me grow my business? If I led my business from somewhere in Ohio driving a Mercedes to the golf course, my business would probably fall apart and I'd miss out on the incredibly rewarding opportunity to upbuild myself and my co-workers. But because I'm here in Valley Center, driving my SUV to the job sites, I'm able to grow my business at least ten times more effectively.

I honestly don't understand how people who run companies like mine can lose touch with their businesses and not bother running them on a day-to-day basis. Frankly, I find that kind of leadership, if you can even call it that, selfish and irresponsible.

All of us on this planet are here to help each other. My employees aren't here just to help me. That's not the kind of company I want to run. I want to be just as valuable to my co-workers and customers as they are to me. The relationships I have with everyone involved in my businesses have to be mutually beneficial, so all of us can achieve the highest possible degree of success together as a team.

For me, being a hands-on leader makes it easier to make decisions, solve problems, and adapt to changes. I always know what's going on at my company, and this enables me to understand what people are talking about when questions or problems arise and to make quick, informed decisions that can save us time and money and move us into profitable new directions.

As the leader of Michael Crews Development, one of my responsibilities is to think ahead about two to five years. Many of the issues that I personally work on now are the things that my business will be working on in two to five years. I'm always thinking about new techniques that can improve our processes, looking for new amenities that people are going to want, and watching for new trends in home building. By staying hands-on with everything in my business on a day-to-day basis, I'm better able to look to the future, set the right goals for the company, and guide the business on a smooth course toward continued success.

Imagine if I didn't know what my people were doing. I'd be likely to accuse them of not doing their jobs correctly, blame them for my problems, and cause them to hate their jobs. I wouldn't be doing much upbuilding, and I sure wouldn't be relaxing and seeing the big picture.

I believe that everyone in leadership positions should know what the people around them are doing. How can you possibly lead effectively if you're not in the know? In my opinion, some of the best leaders are people who literally worked their way up to the top, gaining appreciation for everything that it takes to run a business along the way.

Even if you come into a business that's new to you and somehow start right at a top level of management, it's important to get an understanding of all the job functions in your company. I even suggest that you volunteer to do some of the less glamorous jobs from time to time yourself, just to help you stay connected with every part of your company and to help you appreciate the importance of every task in your company's overall achievement.

Besides the knowledge I gain about my business, being a hands-on leader helps me attract and create hard workers. People want to perform for a great coach. Being that type of leader, I can put together a team that's made up of the best people and create a strong and stable company. Having a stable company of long-term employees has contributed a great deal to the success of my business. As a business leader, you don't want to be working with new faces all the time. You want to keep the people you're working with happy, you want to invest in their skills, and you want to upbuild them instead of knocking them down, in part because training new people costs time and money. People with a history in a business can save that business time and money, because they've mastered the details and know how to prevent and deal with problems.

Hands-on leadership is also a lot of fun. As you've probably figured out by now, I get great satisfaction from being actively engaged in my work, from achieving my goals, and from thinking creatively with a team of hard workers. Working hard and leading others gives purpose to my life.

Being a hands-on leader also benefits the people I work with. People want to know that what they're doing is important, they want their work to be appreciated, and they want a leader who can show them how to be the best they can be. They get all these things from hands-on leaders who work hard themselves and give their employees the tools they need to succeed—like motivation, confidence, and a sense of dedication to the team.

If I walked into the office or onto the job site and wasn't energetic, or if I didn't encourage and empower my employees, then I'd be defeating my own purpose as a leader. Interacting with the people who work with me and being there to offer help, advice, and support is important for me and for them. It's also big when I can be there to celebrate with my team and say congratulations and thank you to them with sincerity. Being hands-on gives me a greater appreciation of all the challenges my co-workers face and all the triumphs my co-workers experience.

Being a hands-on leader means never managing by fear. That goes completely against the idea of upbuilding and pushes people away from you. I'll always find time to listen to anyone in my company, and if there's a problem I'll work with them to find a solution. The people who work with me know that I'm always there for them. They know that they're in a safe, nurturing environment with a leader who's looking out for their needs and who respects them.

When you're a hands-on leader, your hard work also becomes an example for everyone in the work environment. This empowers other people to work hard and make good decisions of their own. When the people who work with me see how much I care about my business and how important a good work ethic is to me each and every day, they tend to care more and work harder, too. And when you know that your employees care and are committed to working hard, you trust them more and give them greater responsibilities. It's a circle of hard work and trust that's the engine for building successful teams and successful businesses.

When I'm involved in my business and my co-workers are thriving because of my hands-on involvement, my customers benefit, too. They benefit from a productive and efficient team of hard workers doing everything they can to produce a quality product.

Anyone in any company can be a hands-on leader. Hands-on leadership is less about a position, a title, a corner office, or a reserved parking place than it is about having respect for yourself and others. If you haven't figured it out already, adopting the characteristics of a hard worker sets you up to be a leader in your place of business, no matter what your current position.

There are lots of things you can do to become a hands-on leader right now. You can set an example of hard work that can inspire the people who work with you and around you. You can master the details of your job and share your knowledge to help your co-workers do their jobs better. You can set goals that make you and your team more productive and efficient. You can think

creatively. You can upbuild your co-workers and foster camaraderie in the workplace. You can hold yourself accountable for
the work you do. And you can relax in the face of problems and
take a big-picture view of your business. These are qualities of
leaders.

And you can do any of the other things mentioned in this
chapter. You can listen to problems. You can help people find
solutions. You can offer encouragement and celebrate people's
successes. You can think about the future of your business. You
can get in there and get your hands dirty.

18

Define Roles

RUSSELL AHONEN IS IN CHARGE of the dirt. When we build a house, his team gets the land graded and lays in the roads, gutters, and sidewalks. "See you guys," he says when he's done, handing the job over to Moose Cleary, the framing superintendent.

Moose's team covers up all of Russell's work. They put the slab down, lay in rough plumbing and electrical systems, frame the house, and load the roof–everything necessary to get the house ready for framing inspection. "See you guys," Moose says. "I'm gone."

When the client signs off on the framing, Pablo Rivera and his team take over. They cover up everything Moose did. They oversee the lathing and plastering on the outside of the house. Inside, they hang drywall, paint the walls and ceilings, lay tile and flooring, put in cabinets, and install appliances. "See you guys," Pablo says.

Pablo hands the job over to Luis Feria and his team. They cover up all of Pablo's work and put all the finishing touches on the property to make it perfect. They install the drainage system, get the landscaping done, put in driveways, and do a final cleanup of the house and grounds. "See you guys," says Luis.

Next in line is Ralph Capuano, our customer service guy. Ralph and his team get the house ready for the final client walkthrough. They make sure that all the painting touchups are made, that all the light switches work, and that all the upgrades are accounted for. "See you guys," Ralph says.

Ralph hands each house over to me when we're ready to present it to the client. I walk the client through each room, and usually there are big smiles on all our faces. I present the new homeowners with a beautiful bouquet of flowers, hand them their keys, and we all shake hands—sometimes we even hug. "See you guys," I say to my satisfied customers.

All the members of a baseball team know what's expected of them. Pitchers are expected to throw strikes. Outfielders are expected to catch. Big hitters are expected to get big hits. When each individual does his job well, the team has a better chance of winning.

It's the same at Michael Crews Development. All the members of my team have a clear understanding of what they do for the organization and how their jobs are critical to the success of everyone else's job.

Defining roles is especially important at a company like mine, because everyone's always covering up somebody else's work. We dig footings in the ground, and we cover them up with concrete. We cover up the concrete with sticks. We cover up all the electrical, plumbing, and mechanical systems with plaster and drywall. We've got to know that everything is okay with each part of a house before we go covering it up.

In my company, everyone is in charge of a precise area, a precise box, but everybody also has to look out for everybody else. You'll never hear someone say, "That's not *my* job!" at Michael Crews Development. Even though roles are strictly defined, best practices dictate that we all work together by sharing our knowledge and helping each other out. People here are motivated to do their jobs right and watch out for other people's work at the same time, and that's a pretty neat thing.

Think about your own job situation or that of some of your co-workers and friends. If they're not looking out for everyone else and working as hard as they can to do their best at their own tasks, then the entire organization suffers. The suffering may not be felt directly, but it's there. It's there in the low morale. It's there in the lackluster productivity. It's there in the low energy. It can be there and people might not even realize it, because that's how it's always been and people don't expect more.

As an employee, I've always wanted to know what's expected of me on the job. And as a manager, I've learned that most people feel the same way.

A clear definition of roles and responsibilities gives hard work a chance to thrive. If I know what's expected of me, I can master the details. I can prevent problems and handle them more efficiently. I can share my expertise with my team. I can take on more responsibility when I get so good at my current job that it becomes almost second nature.

When you have a team of hardworking experts doing the best they can do at their specific tasks, you have a team with a much better chance of winning the game of business.

My unique system of building puts all of our superintendents on all of our houses. Most builders stick one superintendent on a job site and say, "This is your job. Get it built, get it out of here, and get the client's money." Instead, we have everybody involved. We each have our jobs to do, and we do them right because we work as a team. The same is true in our sales department. When we sell a house, all the salespeople share the commission. That way, everyone is motivated to do their job to the best of their ability, and everyone is also motivated to help each other out.

Whenever we build and sell a house, each team works as hard as they possibly can, knowing that they're turning the house over to another team that's equally important in the process. There's a real spirit of cooperation here—among all of our employees and outside contractors—that says I'm going to do my job to the best of my ability so that the next person in line can do his or her best with minimal problems.

And if there are any problems, my guys and gals know where to go—to the folks who had the job before them, or to the people they're going to turn the job over to. People who find a problem will go to the people who had the job before them and ask for help before it gets too far out of hand. And people who know that they've caused a problem will talk to the people who get the job next and help them figure out a solution.

There aren't a lot of layers at my company. There's no bureaucracy. If someone needs to get something done or corrected, all they have to do is call the right person.

When the process works the way it's designed to work, it's truly a wonderful experience. When everyone has a specific job to do, and when everyone knows that how well they do their job affects everyone else's work, people work harder and more efficiently. I'm reluctant to compare this system to an assembly line because that seems so impersonal, but that's really the kind of awesome efficiency and productivity it generates. Defining roles keeps us on top of all our projects, allows us to build faster, and helps us maintain incredibly high quality standards. It allows the people who work here to master the details of their jobs and do what they do best.

When I see the smiling face of a customer, I know that my entire team has supported me in the creation of that smile. Every team member is responsible for that outpouring of joy that occurs when a customer moves into his or her new home and sees that everything is absolutely perfect.

We explain our unique way of doing things to every prospective employee who comes to interview for a job at Michael Crews Development. And when job candidates realize what this means in terms of working together as a team and how different this philosophy is from other companies, it's usually one of the most important reasons they want to work here.

If you're a manager at a company, I recommend that you define specific roles for your team players. I also recommend that you teach everyone you manage how to work together by first working as hard as possible to get their own job done right, and then by helping each other if and when any problems arise.

If you're not a manager, define your own role and see how it fits together with the jobs of other people in your company. You may even want to talk to your manager about how your team can more effectively define roles that allow each person to make the entire team stronger.

It's an important exercise for any business, because a team of hard workers is usually greater than the sum of its parts.

Hire People Smarter Than You

MIKE WUNDERLIN WAS STUDYING the map, and a puzzled look crossed his face.

Mike, who's been working with me since day one, is the most brilliant guy in the world when it comes to engineering. When I saw him looking at the map, I knew he was either going to save me some money, make one of my developments safer, or both.

"What's this section of road doing here?" he asked me, pointing to an 800-foot stretch of road in the fourth phase of a big development called Sky Ridge Estates.

I looked at the map.

"You don't need it," he said.

He was right. That part of the road was absolutely unnecessary.

Mike made a few little adjustments, and saved my company about $400,000.

Now that's smart!

When you're a manager or a business owner, you have to hire people to help you run your business. This is one of the most difficult things to do. It costs a lot of money and time to get people on board and bring them up to speed. So you want to make sure that you're getting the best and brightest people, who'll work hard at your company for a long time.

My best advice is to always hire people who are smarter than you. Always. If a person you're interviewing for a job is not smarter than you are, then you don't want him or her.

In my case, it's pretty easy for me to find people who are smarter than I am. But I'm really the smart one because I'm hiring people who are smarter than me.

Some people feel threatened by people who are smarter than they are. They're afraid that a new, smarter person in the workplace is going to take over their job or find a way to get rid of them. That has no place in a company that's run as a team where everyone helps everyone else, and it goes against all the principles of hard work that we've talked about so far.

If smarter people intimidate you, think about how you constantly hire smarter people in other aspects of your life. Every time you go to the grocery store, to the dentist, to the auto mechanic, or to the bank, you're hiring people who are smarter than you in their particular areas of expertise. Are you threatened by these people? Of course not.

The same idea works at work. You want to surround yourself with smart, hardworking people who can inspire others (including yourself) to work harder, too.

Even though I'm a hands-on leader who enjoys staying involved in all the details of my businesses, it takes a lot of pressure off me to know that smart people are doing every job in the entire company. I don't have to get involved in fixing problems as much as I'd have to if I hired dumb people.

I'm the kind of leader who wants to check on problems. But if there are too many problems to check on, I can't perform my other important responsibilities—like planning for the future of the business, setting goals, and upbuilding co-workers. If I have lots of smart people working for me, the fewer problems I'm going to have, and the more fun I'll have as a leader by being able to celebrate the achievements of my team.

Everyone at Michael Crews Development—and at all the other businesses I'm involved with—is smarter than me.

The people on the Development Team and the A-Team are absolutely phenomenal. The people running our bank are absolutely phenomenal. The people running our mortgage company are absolutely phenomenal. On and on it goes, and I couldn't be more pleased with all the smart, hardworking people I have all around me.

I absolutely love finding smart people to hire. There was a time, for example, when we used to use the services of an outside escrow company. A woman named Tammy Dalbey worked with us quite a bit, and people kept telling me how great she was to work with. After more and more great reports, and after getting to know her better, I asked her if she'd ever thought about running her own company. When you see talent like that, you just want to snag it so that none of your competitors gets a chance to use it.

"Well, yes, I have," she said. "But I don't know how I'd set one up. Plus, I don't have the money to get something like that off the ground."

"Let's go," I said, and together we opened Diamond Escrow Inc. I hired another person smarter than me, and gave Tammy an opportunity she may not have otherwise gotten.

The same goes for Mike Wunderlin, the super-smart engineer. I've been working with him for 23 years, but it took me 21 years before I could keep him to myself and prevent other developers from benefiting from his talents.

When Mike and I first met, we were both starting our own businesses. If you remember, Mike helped me divide my first piece of investment property into two lots so I could put another house on the land. When Art and I got our business going and needed engineering work done, we always called Wunderlin Engineering because Mike was so good, so smart, and so hard-working.

Mike Wunderlin worked for about ten developers besides us, and had built up a good business for himself. But after awhile, Michael Crews Development was growing so fast that he couldn't keep up with our projects. I told him that he should give up his other clients and work exclusively for us. We needed him to keep up or we'd have to hire another person to do part of the work, and I really wanted to give all of our work to him.

Initially, he resisted the offer. He didn't want to end his relationships with his other clients, and he wasn't sure if putting all his eggs in one basket was a good idea. I worked hard for six months to convince him. I explained to him that he'd make more money working for us than he did on his own. I told him that in return for his services and half ownership of the engineering company, he'd also be my partner in some development deals.

Two years ago, Mike and I opened Emerald Crest Engineering and Emerald Crest Development II, and both of us have benefited tremendously from our association. Under normal conditions, it takes about three years to get an engineering package done for a new development, complete with biological impact studies, traffic flow studies, surveys, drawings, etc. But now, with Mike on our team exclusively, we can get a complete engineering package done in less than two years. In fact, not a job goes by that Mike doesn't make better, safer, quicker, or less expensive. He's a smart guy and I'm glad he's on our side!

Mike Wunderlin and Tammy Dalbey are just two examples of how hiring people smarter than you can help you achieve even greater success. If you're ever in a position to hire someone or choose someone to work with you in any capacity, make the smart decision and pick someone smarter than you are.

20

Give People What They Need To Succeed

ONE OF THE FIRST THINGS my wife Kelly did when she started working with me in 1998 was tell me that we needed a new copy machine.

"Are you kidding me?" I said. "The copier we have is just fine."

"It takes forever to make one copy," she grumbled.

"I've had that machine forever!" I replied.

"And you can tell it's from the Stone Age. Have you noticed how long people have to wait in line just to use it? We need something that's a lot faster."

"Do you know how much a new copier costs?" My cheap side was taking control of my mouth.

"Do you know how much productivity we're losing by keeping that old machine?"

Kelly persisted, and in the end she convinced me that the need for a new copier justified the expense.

She was right on the money. Getting the new copier drastically changed how things got done in the office. Productivity shot through the roof, and we even outgrew the new machine within a year or two.

It was a hard sell, but I finally bought it. It was the right thing to do for the business and for the administrative team that works so hard to make the business successful.

By the way, my cheap side was placated when I decided to keep the original copier, too. I still use it to this day, and I don't have any plans to get rid of it anytime soon.

———

I t was tough to convince me to get a new copier, but it wasn't difficult to convince me to get a fax machine. I could see right away how that was going to change my business for the better. Back in 1982, my engineer Mike Wunderlin called me up, all excited. "You've got to come over and see this machine I just got!"

"What is it?" I asked.

"You've got to see it to believe it," he replied. "Get over here!"

I went over to his office and saw this big machine that was about the size of a conference table.

"You're not going to believe what this machine can do," Mike said. "I can put in a document, dial a phone number, and the person at the other end gets a copy of the document!"

"No way!" I couldn't believe it.

"It's true!" he said, grinning like a little kid. "It's called a fax machine."

"Where do I get one?"

I ordered one right away, and it instantly streamlined how things got done around the office. I can't believe we ever lived without a fax machine, and I'm beginning to wonder how we ever lived without the Internet and e-mail. Even though real estate development is an old-school business, we use technology to run our operation more efficiently and productively.

Technology is only one of the tools that people need to succeed. There are many others. Some of them are easy to figure out. For example, a framer needs a hammer, some sticks, and some nails. He wouldn't be able to do too much with a saw, some metal, and some masking tape.

But other success tools—like our need for a new copier back in 1998—aren't so obvious. Some of them aren't even physical things. The good manager, and the good co-worker, listens to people, finds out what they need, and gets it for them. The good manager upbuilds people by giving them the tools they need to succeed.

That's what I tried to do in Poway when I first had the opportunity to manage a real estate office. I gave my agents lots of things they needed to turn jobs they hated into careers they could love, work hard at, and get ahead with.

In my opinion, there are universal tools for success that any person doing a job can benefit from, and many of them don't cost anything. You'll find these things throughout this book, but in this chapter I wanted to focus your attention on some of the most important ones.

The first tool that I believe people need to succeed is motivation—the spark of energy that inspires them to work hard. I've found that people are motivated when they have goals they can buy into. And they get even more motivated when the achievement of those goals leads to some kind of recognition or reward. When I became the manager of the real estate office in Poway, I set goals and I created contests and incentives to motivate the agents. Every month, there'd be something going on. Sometimes it would be a dinner for two for the month's top-selling agent.

Other times it would be a group trip to a ball game if we met our monthly goal as an office. We even had reverse contests—the three worst-selling agents each month had to share a desk.

You may think that competitive motivation works against camaraderie at work, but it's actually the exact opposite. All hard workers appreciate healthy competition, and can see the big picture enough to be happy for other hard workers who win the internal contests and to simply try harder next time.

The second tool that people need to succeed is confidence— the belief in their ability to do their jobs well and take on more responsibility to get ahead. Confidence is developed through the achievement of attainable goals. You can help people achieve their goals when you show them what's expected of them, make sure they know how to do their jobs, and tell them that their work is important. People are also more likely to achieve their goals— and become more confident—when you give them positive words of encouragement, are around to answer questions, and stay calm when they make mistakes.

The third tool that people need to succeed is dedication—the willingness to work hard because it's personally rewarding and because it enriches the lives of others. This ties back into the goals that motivate people to succeed in the first place, and is enhanced by good pay and frequent rewards, camaraderie in the workplace, and the continuous accumulation of satisfied customers.

When people have motivation, confidence, and dedication, they become unstoppable hard workers. They become ready to master the details of their jobs. They strive to perform at their best because they want to be part of a winning team. They upbuild themselves from within because they know that the people around them are upbuilding them from without. They become accountable for their work because they believe in the company's goals and are encouraged and rewarded for their efforts. They become creative problem solvers. They relax and see the big picture, because they're committed. And, best of all, they'll develop into hands-on leaders who give even more people the tools they need to get ahead.

It should be obvious what's going on here. The things other people need to succeed are the same things you need to succeed, too.

21

Offer Encouragement

COACH CARLOSKI WAS A SCREAMER.

"Don't throw it inside–throw it outside!"

He constantly yelled at me while I was on the pitcher's mound in my senior year of high school.

"Get it lower, Crews!"

If I didn't pitch absolutely perfectly, he'd yell at me. This was not the way to get me to play my best. It would rattle me big-time.

After one particularly stressful game, when coach Carloski was particularly loud and obnoxious and I was particularly frustrated, my dad approached him. "Let me tell you something about my kid," he said. "He'll go to bat and die for you, but you've got to leave him alone."

Coach Carloski was angry with my dad for talking to him like that. And he was angry with me for pitching poorly that day. But against all his instincts, the next time I was on the mound he bit his tongue.

And that day I threw a one-hitter.

Coach Carloski couldn't believe it. He went up to my dad and said, "Thank you, Mr. Crews. I was too close to the situation to see what I was doing to Mike."

"Yelling doesn't work for Mike," my dad said. "But he really thrives on encouragement."

E very chance I get, I try to say something positive to the people who work with me. Even when someone's not doing the greatest job in the world, I do my best to offer encouragement. In fact, I think it's especially important to encourage people when they're struggling with something, because that's when they're the most vulnerable. Rather than criticize someone, acknowledge the difficulty they're going through and reassure them that it's not insurmountable. You can help someone overcome a problem by pointing out some of their past successes. You can remind them of the reasons they were hired in the first place. You can tell them that you have faith in them. And you can assure them that challenges are learning experiences that will help them in the future. Positive words of encouragement are powerful confidence builders.

In addition to finding good things to say about others, I give myself encouragement on a regular basis. At the end of each day, I review my working hours and congratulate myself for all the things that went well. Then I think about what I need to do tomorrow and give myself a little pep talk. This little exercise takes about 20 minutes—I can do it while I'm driving home—and it really helps me increase my productivity and efficiency. It may sound corny, but it works!

Encouraging people doesn't cost anything, but the simple act of saying something positive can yield huge dividends for any business. Like goals, words of encouragement are especially effective if they're said out loud and in public. If you say sincere, positive things about people in front of their peers, it puffs them up and makes them work harder to succeed.

Praise is so good for company morale that I try to make public declarations of kudos whenever possible. At every weekly meeting, during every visit to a job site, or whenever else I have the opportunity, I single out the people who're doing an exceptionally good job and tell them how much I appreciate it. In my company's quarterly newsletter (which is actually a 16-page, full-color, glossy magazine), we constantly shine the spotlight on individuals who contribute the most to the excellence our customers have come to expect.

Praise is one of the easiest and best ways to upbuild people. I've been giving Sam Hernandez a lot of compliments recently, not only because he deserves them, but also because I'm trying to get him more comfortable in his new role as our custom home superintendent. He's definitely getting there through his enthusiasm and hard work. My clients are telling me that he's doing well, and I want everyone on the Development Team to know that I keep getting good reports about him. Naturally, this makes Sam feel good, and it helps give him the motivation, confidence, and sense of commitment he needs to become a regular Cougar killer.

Sam's story is similar to Moose Cleary's. Sam had been framing houses for Michael Crews Development for about 12 years, and now he's working hard to master a whole new set of details in a position that gives him more responsibility.

With custom homes, there are lots of details to master. For each house, people are picking out every doorknob, switch, cabinet, and appliance. The appliances alone create all kinds of challenges that affect the building process. Different appliances have different power wattages and different dimensions, so we need to know everything the client wants before we can start building.

And once Sam has all the information he needs in front of him, he has to sit down and figure out how to make it all work as efficiently as possible. It can be overwhelming, but Sam has our entire team cheering him on.

Studies have shown that most people are willing to work for less money in return for more respect and appreciation at work. That's startling! I don't use encouragement as a replacement for money, but these studies illustrate how important praise really is to most people.

People thrive on recognition and encouragement, and it amazes me to think that there's even one coach Carloski out there— on the playing field or in the workplace. Is it really a secret that everyone responds to simple expressions like "Thank you!" "Congratulations!" and "Good job!" from the people around them?

My success, and the success of Michael Crews Development, couldn't have been achieved without the hard work and commitment of each employee, contractor, and supplier who works with us. The efforts of these people to consistently contribute 150% to the job at hand is a gift I cherish every single day, and I want them all to know it as often as possible.

22

Reward Achievement Generously

"HOW ARE YOU GUYS ever going to top this?"

That's what everyone asked Kelly and me after we took about 25 members of the Development Team and the A-Team–along with their spouses, significant others, or best friends–on a one-week cruise to Tahiti.

The Tahiti trip was well deserved, although it was late. We were supposed to go to Tahiti in December of 2001, but world events changed our plans.

The 9/11 tragedy shut down the housing market in North County. We kept building, but we weren't selling. We decided not to cut back, not to lay anyone off, even though our inventory was piling up. We pretended as best we could that everything was okay, and we had faith that things would eventually turn around.

And they did. November and December were good months. People were buying houses again. We made a new goal for the middle of 2002, and by spring we knew that we'd be able to meet it.

Determined to reward my team for working so hard in such a tough time, we planned a new trip for March of 2002. It was going to be a once-in-a-lifetime vacation for a lot of the people on my team.

We went as a group, but I encouraged everyone to do their own thing. Although I'm a great boss, I didn't want anyone to feel like they had to hang out with me the whole time.

We did, however, decide to have dinner together each night. And by the time the last evening rolled around, when all of us were well fed, happy, rested, and ready to tackle the world when we got home–everyone could honestly ask Kelly and me, "How are you guys ever going to top this?"

Words of encouragement and praise are rewards that you can give hard workers every day, but I believe that you need to reserve other types of rewards for special occasions.

These are rewards with some weight to them. I liken them to the Stanley Cup in hockey or to The Oscar in the film industry. They're the kinds of rewards that tell people that their hard work is appreciated. They can be extravagant, like trips to Tahiti, or they can be simple, like a reserved parking space for a top sales-person, a $100 check, or the Quota Buster Awards I received when I started selling real estate. Just as people love to hear words of praise, everyone loves a trophy, a bonus, a dinner, a trip, a plaque, or any other tangible symbol that declares them a winner.

I have a few rules about rewards that I follow as often as possible. My first rule is that an average guy doing an average job is nothing you want to reward. I reward pretty heavily, but the rewards have to be earned through superior performance. My second rule is that you should always reward the people you work with, plus their spouses, significant others, or best friends.

Doing this does two things. It tells your co-workers that you know they have a life outside the workplace, and it shows their spouses, significant others, or best friends that all the long nights and crazy hours they have to put up with are valued. Finally, my third rule is to reward hard workers as much as possible, because rewards are as much fun to give as they are to get.

There are several types of rewards that the hard workers at Michael Crews Development receive throughout each year. There are rewards that motivate people to achieve specific goals. There are rewards that are won through healthy, spirited competition. There are rewards that everyone in the company enjoys. And there are rewards that take people completely by surprise.

All rewards are motivating, but the most motivating rewards tend to be the ones that people receive for achieving a goal, and the ones that people have to compete for. These types of rewards really get people to work hard. My Quota Buster Awards and our Tahiti trip are perfect examples. I was extremely motivated to beat Tommy Hopkins' record, and the Quota Buster Award was a symbol of that accomplishment. And everyone on the Development Team and the A-Team busted their butts to achieve our annual sales goal, in part because they wanted a once-in-a-lifetime cruise to Tahiti.

The rewards we give for achieving our annual sales goals are significant. I like offering exotic trips, because they create fond memories and build camaraderie. Trips are a lot of fun, but they have a downside. They can be hard to coordinate, and scheduling problems, illnesses, and accidents inevitably prevent a few people from being able to go. When this happens, I usually give the people who can't come along something else to show my appreciation for their work.

Because trips can get complicated, we don't offer them all the time. Other times the reward is money. A cash reward may not

create the same kind of camaraderie a trip does, but it sure motivates employees to do their best. Money is good because everyone can enjoy it whenever and however they want to.

Another reward that the employees of Michael Crews Development work hard for is the Leadership Award. It's a lot less
extravagant than the trips and cash we give for reaching our
annual sales goals, but in many ways it's a lot more meaningful.
Every person in the entire company is eligible to receive the Leadership Award, but it's only presented to a single individual each
year at our Christmas party. (The year 2000 was an exception—
Mary Bradley and Moose Cleary both won that year.)

It's a big honor to win the Leadership Award, which in many
ways is the equivalent of an MVP award in sports. The Leadership Award at Michael Crews Development symbolizes extraordinary achievement from someone who's already part of an
extraordinary team, and it's always a tough choice. Everyone in
the company votes for the person they think should receive the
award for the year, and Kelly and I use the results to pick the ultimate winner. Then, at our Christmas party, we announce the winner and pay tribute to that person in front of everybody in the
company. It really is a big deal.

The Leadership Award is an etched glass diamond that stands
about a foot high, and it sits proudly on the desks and in the offices
of the people who've won it over the years. These amazing people, who are hard workers to begin with, somehow find ways to
work even harder because they value that reward so much.

Still motivational, but less specific and not at all competitive
are the rewards our company gives to celebrate hard work in general. The best example of this type of reward is the Christmas
party we throw each year for all of our employees and their
guests. Everyone who's a part of my business gets to come and
bring a date. We have a great dinner, there's terrific music, and we
pat each other on the back for a great year. We always make a

presentation at the party that highlights some of the year's triumphs, and we use the successes and challenges of the year to inspire everyone to work hard in the year ahead.

The last reward type I want to discuss is the kind of unexpected reward that people get for just being wonderful hard workers. These rewards also run the gamut from the simple to the extraordinary. On one end, you've got things like Luis's new, cherried-out pickup truck, and on the other end you've got things like a bouquet of flowers or an impromptu lunch for a hardworking landscaping crew.

These surprise rewards are like words of encouragement on steroids. Even the small surprises are huge. I know because I've experienced them myself. You may remember the story about my team in Poway who hired a tennis instructor for me and wrote a funny poem about their respect for me as a manager. Things like that mean a great deal to me, and make me work harder to benefit my team.

Just this past year, everyone at Michael Crews Development threw me a barbecue lunch for my birthday, and that was huge to me. It was a small thing that was huge. It told me that my employees like me, want to be with me, and want to learn from me. That's big-time motivation for me to work as hard as I possibly can.

I like giving surprise rewards because the reactions from the people receiving them are so much fun to watch. These reactions also reveal a great deal about the character of the hard worker. The initial reaction is always one of utter shock and disbelief—as if the person receiving the reward doesn't believe that he or she deserves it. Hard workers tend to downplay their own accomplishments and are somewhat embarrassed by lavish displays of appreciation. But at the same time, you can see in their faces how much it means to them to be appreciated, even if they would have gotten along fine without any special recognition.

I believe that rewarding achievement generously is absolutely necessary for managers of hard workers. Whether it's a plaque, a dinner, a trip, or a bonus, a tangible marker of achievement gives the hard worker even more confidence and even more energy to continue doing his or her best. And it's just simply a nice thing to do to show someone how highly you think of them and how much you value their individual contribution to the team effort.

Rewards are such a big deal at Michael Crews Development that we even reward our customers. Whenever we hand over a house to a customer, they also get a big, beautiful bouquet of flowers. It's just our way of rewarding them for working hard with us to build the house of their dreams. They appreciate the thank you, and they constantly tell me that they really feel like they're part of the Michael Crews Development family. We benefit too, because this small token of appreciation helps turn our customers into some of the best PR and advertising people around.

Rewards are wonderful tools for hard workers. They build confidence and camaraderie, they develop pride and accountability, they motivate people to work harder, they create lasting memories, and they make hard work a lot more fun.

23

Play Hard

PABLO WON $500.

I won $250.

There were other winners, but that's not the real reason I took the Development Team and the A-Team (and their spouses, significant others, or best friends) to Las Vegas for two days.

I joked that we were going to Vegas because I was tired of eating at The Brigantine, the nice steak house where we usually have our meetings every three months. But that wasn't the real reason we were going to Vegas, either.

Everybody wanted to know why we were going to Las Vegas.

All 77 of us met at the airport, hopped a flight, and got to Vegas at about 11:00 a.m.

After we checked into the Bellagio, we were free to do our own thing all afternoon. Some people lounged around the pool, some went shopping, some drove all around town, and some went straight to the casinos.

We met back at the hotel for a fantastic dinner, and then took in the amazing show, "O." Our seats were really close to the stage, and some of them were so close they were in what they called the "Wet Zone."

It was a jam-packed day full of fun, and it was great to be away from the office.

The next day, we had more free time and headed to the airport in the afternoon to catch our flight back home.

We needed this trip to Vegas.

We had just over three months to achieve our annual sales goal, and we needed to do a little whooping to fire everyone up for the final push. We also wanted to make sure everyone had some fun with their spouses and friends, because when we got back we'd be busier than we'd been all year.

Everyone had a great time, there was a ton of camaraderie, and we got back ready to work harder than ever.

That's why we went to Las Vegas.

———————

When you work really, really hard, you get to play really, really hard. Play makes work a lot more fun and helps people recharge their batteries.

There are two types of play that I want to talk about. The first is the kind of play that directly builds camaraderie in the workplace, and the second is the kind of play that has absolutely nothing to do with work at all.

You already know how critical I believe camaraderie is for a business to be successful. I told you how I built camaraderie back in my 20s to turn around the dying real estate office in Poway, by encouraging playful activities like dressing up as hillbillies for a meeting at another real estate office. And I told you how I build camaraderie at Michael Crews Development by throwing parties, ordering impromptu lunches, and taking people to places like Tahiti and Las Vegas.

I bring up the importance of camaraderie so often because camaraderie in the workplace is essential to both individual and team success. Camaraderie leads to superior performance and achievement. Camaraderie creates a bond among co-workers, and makes working fun. And when work is enjoyable, people tend to work harder and achieve more, and that achievement makes work even more fun. Play is a huge way to build camaraderie.

We play on a daily basis. We goof around a lot, we joke with each other, we laugh together, and we genuinely enjoy being around each other. We'll go out to lunch together, we'll celebrate people's birthdays, and we'll spend time talking about our families and current events.

This type of everyday play makes our daily tasks less mundane and prepares us for the times when we really need to focus hard on work—whether we're getting ready for the last rush toward achieving a goal, or whether we're trying to prevent a problem from getting out of hand. We can be serious when we need to be, but there's no reason to be serious all the time. All work and no play makes Michael Crews Development employees dull boys and girls, and dull is no way to be if you want to get ahead.

People who play together tend to get along with each other better, and that keeps morale problems to a minimum. Companies have morale problems when people start slacking off, but we have so much camaraderie at Michael Crews Development that everyone wants to do their best work to help everyone else in the office do *their* best work. Nobody here slacks off and everybody gets along—so we're always in a good mood! We come to the office or go to the job site to work hard, but it's not worth it if we're not having a good time.

Playing hard means not taking ourselves too seriously. It means dressing up as hillbillies and making up silly poems about each other. Making fun of yourself and the people you work with is a great way to build camaraderie, because you can only poke fun at people you love and respect and get away with it. And you can only poke fun at someone who's confident enough to know that you're just playing around. When you're part of a solid team and make fun of someone on that team, you know they're going to take it in the good-natured spirit in which it is always meant. Trust me, I have no tolerance for mean-spirited name-calling or cruel jokes of any kind.

I encourage my team to make fun of who we are and what we do in positive ways. We made a video one year for our Christmas party, which made people laugh so hard I thought the roof in the banquet hall was going to cave in. Part of the video showed Ralph, our customer service guy, pretending to insult our customers on the phone. "You're beyond warranty" was Ralph's catch phrase as he talked to imaginary customers on-camera. It was Ralph's way of poking fun at my insistence on perfection, which everyone knows he totally believes in. We could laugh at Ralph, and at ourselves, because we know that he's incapable of being rude to any of our real customers—just like the rest of us.

When you can have some fun at the office, watch morale go up and watch your productivity soar.

As much as the hard worker loves working and has fun working, it's good to get completely away from the office now and then. I'll admit that it took a long time for me to get to that way of thinking.

In the beginning, I never used to play much outside of the office. I was so focused on building my career that I really didn't have time to even think about taking time off. All of my time and energy was put into my jobs and my businesses. That was really fun for me, and I played really hard within the work environment, but I think I probably missed out on some quality time with my family in the early days.

When I finally started taking vacations, I'd go away for two or three weeks at a time. That was a big mistake, because I'd be so overwhelmed with work when I got back that all the benefits of my vacations soon vanished.

I realized that big vacations weren't working for me, so now I do things a little differently. I go away more often, but only for a few days at a time. I never go away longer than a week.

It's still hard for me to take time off, but I know that I need to do it. First and foremost, the time away from the job really makes me appreciate my family. I recently went to a dude ranch in the middle of nowhere. I had the opportunity to see my three-year-old daughter Sky get attached to a horse named Freckles. And Kelly and I had some of the best conversations we've ever had with Ashley and Justin. It was real heart-to-heart, deep stuff that you can only have when there's absolutely nothing to distract you.

In addition to helping you connect with your family and friends, playtime away from the office can also give you a new perspective on your job. Sometimes, a trip will make me miss working so much that I develop an even stronger appreciation for my work ethic and the career I've created for myself. Other times, I'll forget about work so completely that I'll get back to work and be able to effortlessly solve problems that I was struggling with before. And sometimes I'll get so inspired from a change of scenery that I come back full of new ideas.

Leaving the office for a few days every now and then recharges my batteries so I can hit the ground running when I get back to work.

24

Serve The Greater Good

A FAMILY BOUGHT A HOUSE from us and it was under construction when their 10-year-old son was diagnosed with leukemia. We let them out of their contract and HOME made a donation to the family. Sadly, this brave little boy lost his battle.

We knew a lady who loved children so much that she ran a day-care facility out of her house in addition to caring for four beautiful little girls of her own. When she was stricken with breast cancer, she continued to work while she was being treated because the children brought her so much joy and happiness. She had to stop working when the cancer spread to her brain. HOME made a contribution to help her make ends meet. Sadly, this lady who loved children never saw them grow up.

Life is a wonderful thing, but it's vulnerable. Every day, we're susceptible to disease, accidents, and acts of violence. While these things are relatively rare in most of our daily lives, none of us are immune to them, and they can strike us down at any time. That's why I believe that it's the responsibility of hard workers everywhere to use their bodies, minds, souls, and financial resources to help others.

A lot has been said about corporate responsibility, and there's certainly a debate about the role that hardworking businesspeople should play in helping the larger community.

I agree with former General Electric CEO Jack Welch, who believes that the only companies that are really in a position to improve and enrich communities are strong, healthy, and profitable companies. He argues that instead of putting restrictions on companies, governments should be upbuilding companies and helping them succeed.

I apply the same logic to individuals. Hardworking, successful individuals are in a much better position to help others than lazy, unsuccessful individuals. Every hard worker has the energy to do something for the greater good, and that capacity grows the more successful one becomes.

Today, I put on my town's Fourth of July celebration, I help people struck by unexpected medical problems, and I donate to various other causes. When I was starting out in the real estate business, I sponsored the printing of little program books for the football games at my old high school. It wasn't a big thing to do, but it helped Orange Glen Patriot fans and players enjoy the games a little more. And in return for paying to print up the programs, I got to run an ad for my real estate business.

Oddly enough, one of the programs I sponsored in 1978— for a game between my Orange Glen Patriots and the San Pasqual Golden Eagles—included pictures of me and my wife Kelly, who was a cheerleader at that time. The funny thing about it was that I wouldn't even meet Kelly for 19 more years!

But I'm getting a little off track here. My point is that the more successful a company or a person becomes, the better able they are to serve the larger community. Strong companies and successful individuals pay taxes, buy goods and services, create jobs, provide products and services that customers want, and abide by the law. Plus, they often have extra money, time, and other resources to help those in need.

As I explained earlier, most of my service for the greater good is centered on the town and county in which I live. The people in this community have been incredibly good to me. They cheered me at my ball games. They challenged me to do better. They buy my houses and wish me well when I see them on the street. I truly enjoy showing my appreciation to the community of people who have made me what I am today.

It's pure pleasure for Kelly and me to put on the Fourth of July celebration and fireworks display at Valley Center High School each year. It gives us great joy to contribute to various local charities. But our biggest love, and our greatest gift to the community, is HOME, the charity we started in 1999.

HOME, which if you remember stands for Helping Others More Efficiently, is a nonprofit corporation that provides assistance to hardworking, employed, productive members of society who are not eligible for government aid, but who—through no fault of their own—find themselves struggling financially with difficult situations. Most of these situations involve major medical traumas that cause financial stress, postpone or even shatter dreams of success, and too often take away valuable human lives.

Since HOME's inception, we've been able to help hundreds of families. It's difficult not to get emotional about it, and all the wonderful people we've helped so far have moved us in a variety of beautiful, sad, touching, and happy ways. Not everyone we help survives, and that's one of the toughest things to deal with because we get so close to them.

Each year, we have a benefit concert to raise money for HOME. We've had country greats like Toby Keith, Tracy Byrd, Brad Paisley, and Diamond Rio, as well as big band leader Bobby Caldwell. We work hard to help families in need, and we have fun in the process.

Kelly and I want our kids to run the charity when they're old enough to take it over, and we hope that it remains a long-lasting legacy of all the hard work we've done in North County. (For more information on how you can help this cause, please call 760-749-1919.)

The path of the hard worker is one of growth and maturity, through which you realize that making money is probably the least important part of being successful. Enriching the lives of your co-workers and customers is more important. But the best part of being successful is feeling so blessed and grateful that you willingly give back to the community of which you are a part.

25

Create Your Own Success Story

YOU'RE JUST ABOUT TO FINISH A BOOK.
Maybe it was a gift from someone who loves you. Maybe you read about it in the newspaper. Or maybe you just saw it at the bookstore or in the library and were compelled to pick it up.

The book's about a guy you've probably never heard of before, but he seems kind of familiar. He's a lot like you–someone with a strong desire to get ahead, someone who wants to be recognized for his efforts, someone who likes to win.

What makes the story interesting is the fact that the guy who wrote it didn't have a lot of the advantages that many people think you need to succeed. He didn't have money, connections, or even an education. All he had was the ability to work hard and the willingness to take pleasure in the work he did, because he knew it would bring him and the people around him incredible benefits.

You probably learned more than you wanted to know about this guy's life and career, about his coaches, his parents, his teachers, his wife, his kids, his employees, and his bosses, but maybe you found the stories entertaining and got some valuable insights and direction from them.

When you put this book down, what are you going to do?

Now it's your turn.

Now it's your chance to lead yourself and others to greatness through your hard work.

There's no better time to start working hard than right now. The sooner you take action, the sooner you can start enriching yourself, your co-workers, your customers, and your community.

What follows is a summary of some of the most important points covered in this book. Refer to this chapter often as you follow the path of hard work toward the success you know you can achieve.

You Know You're A Hard Worker When...

- You work purposefully with focus and vision and always look for new opportunities to enlist the help of other hard workers
- Your actions deliberately minimize risk and maximize the return on your investment of time and energy
- Your actions engage you in your work. When you're involved in something completely, you don't even realize how hard you're working
- Your actions build camaraderie
- You understand that the success of others is tied to your personal success
- You act like a Cougar killer

Find Something To Do

• Productive activity eliminates boredom and frustration. Clean your desk, streamline tasks, and ask for more responsibility

• Avoid busywork, because it doesn't lead to results

• Focus on short-term activities that are true to your long-term vision

• Take on extra jobs to help you get into the habit of working hard. The extra money will motivate you, and the additional commitments will help you set priorities and manage your time better

Use Your Gifts

• When you use your gifts, you can become passionate about any job. I enjoyed delivering water tanks because it gave me the opportunity to prove myself as a salesman

• What are you good at?

　—Think about things you enjoy doing

　—Think about things you enjoyed as a kid

　—Think about things you'd do without pay

　—Ask people who know you what they think would be a good career for you

Master The Details

• When you examine your job under a microscope, you may see how wonderfully complex and interesting it is

• Learn everything you can about your job, and about any other job that has an impact on your work

• The more you understand about what you're doing, the more you'll be able to focus on productivity and efficiency

• If you don't understand what you're doing, ask!

• Mastering the details helps you develop expertise, which, when shared with your teammates, earns you respect and fosters camaraderie and cooperation

• Mastering the details gives you confidence to do more

Upbuild Yourself And Others

- Measured, steady progress is the surest way to incredible success. You may not get where you want to be as quickly as you want to, but you're more likely to get there
- Don't let desire and enthusiasm tempt you to jump too high, and don't let fear, guilt, unworthiness, or strange attitudes about money prevent you from jumping at all
- Upbuilding allows you to be happy in your career and want more at the same time. It's motivation without frustration
- Managers who upbuild others get the best out of everyone who works for them, keep their best people longer, and create new leaders who upbuild others for the benefit of the business
- The easiest way to upbuild someone is to say something positive to him or her

Set Goals You Can Reach

- Goals are roadmaps for upbuilding. They tell you how high you can jump with the highest likelihood of success
- Ask yourself questions—and answer them honestly—to set realistic goals
- Goals that are made public are often easier to achieve
- Achieving goals gives you confidence to try bigger things
- Let skepticism inspire you to anticipate problems and strategize in advance. It feels great to prove skeptics wrong, but make sure you're not striving for a goal just for that reason
- Don't forget dreams—they're your personal vision for your perfect future
- Having big dreams gives you the energy and motivation you need to spark yourself into action. But it's the consistent achievement of smaller goals over time that sustains that energy and allows you to eventually reach your dreams

Be Creative

• Creativity is the mental force that allows you to reach your goals and dreams, no matter what obstacles are stacked against you

• Creativity is free, and it's available in unlimited amounts. As a business resource, it's pure gold

• Making a commitment to work hard can lead you directly toward creative solutions and lucky breaks

• All you have to do to tap into the power of creativity is be open to unconventional solutions, believe that they'll come to you when you need them, and embrace them when they show up

Hold Yourself Accountable

• When you hold yourself accountable, your interactions with co-workers are less stressful. There's more love, camaraderie, and respect in the workplace, and less anger, fear, fatigue, and frustration

• When you hold yourself accountable, you don't have to be afraid of making mistakes because you'll own up to them

• When you hold yourself accountable, you won't waste time criticizing others. You'll be too busy working on the only person you have any control over—yourself

• When you hold yourself accountable, you can look your customers in the eye

Relax And See The Big Picture

• Use these five techniques to keep yourself from getting mad:

—Address problems as soon as they occur

—Accept problems as a cost of doing business

—Turn problems into positives when possible, or at least learn from your problems

—Minimize problems in the first place by mastering the details of your work, upbuilding slowly, and communicating openly

—Count your blessings. Few problems are as disastrous as you think they are

- Think about your job in terms of how it—and your performance at it—impacts real people, including you, your family, your co-workers, your customers, and your community

Be A Hands-On Leader

- Hands-on leadership is beneficial to leaders, their co-workers, and their customers. Get your hands dirty
- Being a hands-on leader makes it easier to make decisions, solve problems, and adapt to change
- Hands-on leaders attract and create other hard workers
- Hands-on leaders never manage by fear. They empower people to work hard and make their own good decisions
- Hands-on leadership is less about a position or title than it is about having respect for yourself and others. Anyone in any business can behave like a hands-on leader by:

    — Setting an example of hard work

    — Sharing expertise with the team

    — Setting goals

    — Thinking creatively

    — Upbuilding themselves and others

    — Building camaraderie

    — Holding themselves accountable

    — Relaxing in the face of problems

    — Listening to and communicating with others

    — Offering praise and celebrating people's successes

Define Roles

• Take charge of your role in your business. Learn what's expected of you so you can master the details, perform at your best, and handle problems efficiently

• Do your job so well that it makes everyone else's job easier and contributes to their success

Hire People Smarter Than You

• Hiring smart people makes you the smart one

• If a person you're interviewing for a job isn't smarter than you are, then you don't want him or her

• The more smart people there are working for you or with you, the fewer problems you'll have, and the more fun you'll have celebrating the achievements of your team

Give People What They Need To Succeed

• Keep up with technology and the latest advances in the physical tools of your trade

• Listen to people, find out what they need, and get it for them

• Don't forget the intangible success tools that I believe are universal:

— Motivation—the spark of energy that inspires people to work hard

— Confidence—the belief in one's ability to do a job well and take on more responsibility

— Dedication—the willingness to work hard because it's personally rewarding and because it enriches the lives of others

Note how the first letters of each of these tools for success are the same as the initials of my company—Michael Crews Development!

Offer Encouragement

- Encouraging people doesn't cost anything, but the simple act of saying something nice can yield huge dividends
- Make public declarations of kudos whenever possible
- People thrive on recognition and encouragement—don't forget to praise yourself, too

Reward Achievement Generously

- Rewards build confidence and camaraderie, develop pride and accountability, motivate people to work harder, create fond memories, and make work more fun
- An average guy doing an average job is nothing you want to reward. Rewards should be earned by superior performers
- When possible, reward spouses, significant others, and best friends along with the people you work with. When I throw a party or take my co-workers on trips I always tell them to bring a friend or a date
- The most motivating rewards tend to be the ones people either compete for or get for achieving a goal
- A reward that comes as a surprise is the ultimate form of encouragement
- Reward hard workers as much as possible, because rewards are as much fun to give as they are to get

Play Hard

- Play at work makes tasks less mundane, builds camaraderie, and prepares you for times when you and your team really need to focus
- Play outside of work lets you enjoy the rewards of your efforts, brings you closer to the people in your personal life, and recharges your batteries so you can continue working hard when you get back

Serve The Greater Good

• The ultimate success is when you feel so blessed and grateful for what your work has built for you that you willingly give back to the community

All it takes to succeed is the decision to become a hard worker, and to use the hard-work actions I've described as you advance along in your career.

You'll be faced with many decisions as you follow the path of the hard worker to success, but my advice is this: Don't dwell on things too long, and don't overthink everything you do. I make decisions very quickly, and I stick with them. I don't always make the right decisions, but I believe that it's usually better to make a wrong decision than no decision at all.

Work purposefully, with the vision of your perfect future always in your mind to guide you. Know that it takes many little steps to complete a long journey, so always focus your complete attention on even the smallest tasks you have to perform. At the same time, look for opportunities—but make sure they really can take you farther before you seize them.

Your destiny is in your own hands. Work hard and you'll succeed. Love yourself and others enough to create your own personal success story. I want to know what happens, so please e-mail me at **michaelc@michaelcrews.com.**

Acknowledgements

Over the years, lots of people have said to me, "Mike, you ought to write a book!" At first I laughed at the idea. Michael Crews write a book? Me?!

But it kept coming up in conversation. Every time I'd run into an old colleague, boss, coach, or friend of mine on the street, they'd ask me when I was going to write that book. Or I'd be talking about one of my experiences, and someone would say, "Gosh Mike, that story could sure inspire a lot of people."

The more this happened, the more I thought that putting my ideas about hard work down on paper might be valuable to people who are frustrated in their careers or looking for a way to get ahead. I thought I could reach a lot of people who needed to learn how to work, especially kids who were just getting started on their careers.

When I began to consider the possibility of telling my story, I soon realized that I didn't know the first thing about writing a book. In fact, I hardly ever used to read books! To be honest, I felt a little intimidated by the project and kept putting it off.

But my friend Clark Bartram kept encouraging me. "You've got to do it!" he'd say. He told me that my story would serve a worthwhile purpose, that my life and work experiences were interesting and inspirational. He told me that if anyone could find a way to write a book about business success, it would be me. He was upbuilding me, and for that I'm extremely grateful.

A well-known fitness personality and an accomplished author himself, Clark took the initiative to get me started. He wrote a few pages about some of the things he knew about my life and career.

Seeing the words actually written out charged me up, and I made writing this book a goal I wanted to achieve.

Clark referred me to a friend of his, Ed Sweet, a writer and editor from Phoenix, Arizona. Ed came out to see me in Valley Center and followed me around for a day. I told him what I wanted to achieve by writing a book, and he asked me a lot of questions about my business, about becoming successful, and about what it means to have a good work ethic. He recorded our conversations and used them to lay the foundation for a full-length book. Ed really got into my head and helped me crystallize my ideas. He also made me dig deep for some of the stories included in these pages.

Many of the stories came from my own memory, but I had to ask around for others. My mom and dad, Ken and Erlene Crews, were valuable sources of information, and it was fun reliving some of our past experiences together. Talking about my childhood with them reminded me how much I love them and how much they've meant to me over the years.

Additional stories and information came from other key people in my life, and I want to thank them for their help. These wonderful people include my wife Kelly, my best friend Art Duncan,
my first full-time boss Knox Williams, my hardworking sales
director Mark Connal, and my assistant Mary Bradley. Mary also
took on the huge responsibility of verifying every name, date,
and number in the book, and for that I'm extremely grateful.

I'm also grateful to my parents for digging out their old scrap-
books and photo albums and contributing photos for the center
section of the book. It was a fun trip down memory lane.

Speaking of photographs, I have to give kudos to Garrett
Delph of Garrett Photography in San Diego for taking such a great
picture of me for the cover. He had his work cut out for him, but,
in addition to having an amazing work ethic and an amazing talent, he brought in Misty Casas, a hardworking hair and makeup
artist, and Brooks Ray, a hardworking photo assistant to pull it all
off. Garrett's another friend of Clark Bartram's, and he's one of the
nicest and most creative people I've ever met. He really made me
look like I was comfortable in front of the camera.

Lots of other creative people contributed to *Hard Work*. The
folks at Campbell Fisher Design in Phoenix designed the dust
jacket and the inside photo section. They blew me away right
from the start with about 10 different cover concepts—they were
all so great I had a hard time deciding which one to go with.

Michele DeFilippo of 1106 Design in Phoenix designed the
text for the inside of the book. She's a true craftsperson who has
really mastered the details.

Another detail master is Doran Hunter, who put together the
index. Before I started this project, I didn't even realize that this
job existed. Doran did double-duty on the project. In addition to
creating the index, he proofread the manuscript before it got to
Michele for final typesetting. Kate von Seeburg also proofread
the manuscript. Kate and Doran's fresh, sharp eyes saved us from

embarrassment in a number of places, and their efforts are most appreciated.

I also want to thank David Bennett and David Ferreira, Ph.D., for reviewing the manuscript and giving me lots of great suggestions to make it stronger. My wife Kelly was also a great reviewer and editor. Without her thoughtful guidance, this book could not have been so clear, honest, and entertaining.

I'm indebted to all the people who helped me make this book a reality. Among the most important people are the ones who convinced me to write it in the first place, as well as all the folks who populate its pages. I'm grateful to all my teachers, coaches, teammates, neighbors, friends, bosses, co-workers, customers, and family members who shaped my life in so many significant ways.

I also want to give extra special thanks to my wife and kids for supporting me in this project. They were amazed at how much I really got into it, especially since they've never seen me read a book before.

This book is the result of a lot of hard work from a lot of hardworking people. It stands as a testament to the fact that positive results are easily achievable through hard work.

Lastly, I want to thank you for picking up this book. I appreciate the fact that you've taken the time to learn about my history and study my ideas about work and career success. Writing *Hard Work* has changed my life, and I hope that reading it changes yours.

Index